The Madman of St. James': a narrative, from the Journal of a Physician. Translated from the German, by T. H. vol. II

Philipp Galen, T. H.

The Madman of St. James': a narrative, from the Journal of a Physician. Translated from the German, by T. H.
Galen, Philipp
British Library, Historical Print Editions
British Library
H., T.
1860
3 vol. ; 8??.
12630.b.5.

The BiblioLife Network

This project was made possible in part by the BiblioLife Network (BLN), a project aimed at addressing some of the huge challenges facing book preservationists around the world. The BLN includes libraries, library networks, archives, subject matter experts, online communities and library service providers. We believe every book ever published should be available as a high-quality print reproduction; printed on-demand anywhere in the world. This insures the ongoing accessibility of the content and helps generate sustainable revenue for the libraries and organizations that work to preserve these important materials.

The following book is in the "public domain" and represents an authentic reproduction of the text as printed by the original publisher. While we have attempted to accurately maintain the integrity of the original work, there are sometimes problems with the original book or micro-film from which the books were digitized. This can result in minor errors in reproduction. Possible imperfections include missing and blurred pages, poor pictures, markings and other reproduction issues beyond our control. Because this work is culturally important, we have made it available as part of our commitment to protecting, preserving, and promoting the world's literature.

GUIDE TO FOLD-OUTS, MAPS and OVERSIZED IMAGES

In an online database, page images do not need to conform to the size restrictions found in a printed book. When converting these images back into a printed bound book, the page sizes are standardized in ways that maintain the detail of the original. For large images, such as fold-out maps, the original page image is split into two or more pages.

Guidelines used to determine the split of oversize pages:

• Some images are split vertically; large images require vertical and horizontal splits.
• For horizontal splits, the content is split left to right.
• For vertical splits, the content is split from top to bottom.
• For both vertical and horizontal splits, the image is processed from top left to bottom right.

5

THE MADMAN OF ST. JAMES':

A Narrative,

FROM THE JOURNAL OF A PHYSICIAN.

TRANSLATED

FROM THE GERMAN OF PHILIP GALEN,

By T. H.

IN THREE VOLUMES.

VOL. II.

LONDON:

J. F. HOPE, 16, GREAT MARLBOROUGH STREET.

——

1860.

CONTENTS.

CHAPTER I.

Continuation of the History of the Madman of St. James' 1

CHAPTER II.

Conclusion of the History of the Madman of St. James' 26

CHAPTER III.

Plans for a Bold Undertaking 51

CHAPTER IV.

Departure from St. James' 77

CHAPTER V.

A Tolerably Good Beginning to a Difficult Journey . 88

CHAPTER VI.

A Letter Lost which contains Important News . . 105

CHAPTER VII.

Researches 137

CONTENTS.

CHAPTER VIII.

PAGE

A Celebrated Physician 157

CHAPTER IX.

A Distinguished Patient and a Kind Son . . . 174

CHAPTER X.

The Double Will 211

CHAPTER XI.

Two Doctors to One Patient 249

THE MADMAN OF ST. JAMES'.

CHAPTER I.

CONTINUATION OF THE HISTORY OF THE MADMAN OF ST. JAMES'.

" ONCE more Ellinor and I were sitting together in the green wood; for after dinner her father had left us to ourselves. We conversed about what was, then, the newest and nearest subject to us—about our love—how it had sprung up and increased—how we would prize and cherish it; and then of the future —if it would prove favourable to our wishes.

" The beautiful hours of that lovely, warm summer afternoon seemed almost to fly, and the sun was just setting, when Mr. Graham came to us, and said—

" 'Well, my children, now that you have opened your hearts to each other, give me also a share of your society; but first, I have a few serious words to speak to you alone, Percy.'

" 'What can you have to say to him, my dear father, that I may not hear?' said Ellinor. His weal

VOL. II.   B

and woe are all half mine now; and not only all that
is serious, but all that is sorrowful, I will hear also.
I want my share of everything.'

" ' She is right,' I said; ' as long as I am here I
will not leave her for a moment; for happiness is but
short lived, and when we possess it, the hours fly all
too quickly. What you have to say to me, therefore,
say it in her presence.'

" ' I have no objection,' replied Mr. Graham, ' if
you and Ellinor wish it; and certainly, it concerns her
as much as it concerns you. Now, listen to me; or
perhaps we had better go into the house, for who can
know all the ears and eyes concealed in the wood?'
added he, in a low tone.

" We went home, and seated ourselves in the quiet,
little turret-room, which we liked all the better for
being so quiet.

" ' Have you duly considered, Percy,' began the
good clergyman, ' what effect the event of to-day may
produce in that house yonder?'

" ' Yes, I have considered it,' I answered. ' But
as I am of age, and, as my own master, not as the
heir of the Marquis of Seymour and Earl of Codrington, have asked for Ellinor's hand, the opinion of
my relations on this point must be perfectly indifferent to me. And as a day or so must pass
before the intelligence of our happiness reaches
their ears,'—I forgot at this moment that Mortimer
had witnessed part of it—' there will be time enough

THE MADMAN OF ST. JAMES'. 3

for us to arrange and execute our own plans, so as to be prepared for all efforts that may be made to frustrate them. But, much more than this, my dear Graham, I fear, from what you related to me of your last conversation with my father, that when he learns what has taken place, he is likely to be more irritated against you than against me.'

" 'Do not believe that,' replied Mr. Graham: 'do not for a moment think that. If they are angry, and I do not doubt that fact for a moment, the whole power of their anger will not be turned against any one of us, but against us all.'

" 'Well, then we will quickly decide,' said I. 'And now allow me to make a proposal, which comes from my heart, and, if it meets your approbation, can very quickly be carried out. As long as I am in England, the sun of this land seems rather to burn than to warm me. I know far more tempting lands, where neither strife nor anger can reach us; let us go there, and my fortune, if not the largest in England, is at all events sufficient to provide us there with the means of living quietly, happily, and independently. What do you say, my Ellinor, and you, my dear Graham, to this proposal?'

" Ellinor leaned her head on my shoulder, looking at me in happy silence with a smile, which I believed I understood; but Mr. Graham gravely shook his venerable head, and slowly answered,—

" 'This proposal is a good one for you, my chil-

B 2

dren, but not for me. Shall I leave my quiet home, where I have lived so long, and my flock, which for twenty-four years I have tended and tried to benefit by my services and prayers? And this because I am so weak as to fear insults and injuries, which I may even be spared? Consider it well. Should I not rather go to your father, tell him what has happened, and for my sake, if not for yours, ask his consent? If I am not his dependent, he is still my patron; and besides, Percy, am I not the servant of the church on his estate?'

" 'No, my dear father,' I answered kindly, 'that is not my opinion; and do you consider it well too. To ask him for his consent means to put it out of your power to be able to act on your own judgment as you think right. Let us keep to our first resolution; if you will go to him, because you think it is your duty, wait at least for the time when he himself will summon you, and give you his opinion on the subject.'

" 'That time is not far off, my son,' said Mr. Graham, in a low voice, and he was soon lost in deep thought. I interrupted it by continuing:

" 'Until that time, at least, let us be happy, and quietly make preparations for executing our plans at the shortest notice. To-morrow morning I will, as a preliminary step, send Phillips to Dunsdale, to put everything in readiness. But then, father,'—and my eye rested on Ellinor, who, silent

and blushing, seemed to anticipate my meaning,—
'may I not hope that the fulfilment of my dearest
earthly wish will not be far distant?'

" 'I have nothing to urge against it,' replied Mr.
Graham; 'that is Ellinor's affair, you must consult
her on that point.'

" 'Now, Ellinor,' said I, turning towards her,
'you hear what your father says. I, for my part, will
not hurry you, but circumstances require this haste.
Decide, dearest, and tell me how it shall be.'

" Ellinor looked first at her father, then at me—
for a moment she seemed to reflect, then, however,
instead of answering, she laid her darling head on
my shoulder, and whispered,—

" 'I am ready to act just as you and my father
may wish.'

" 'So be it then,' said he, 'and may He who
dwells above, Who knows all, sees us, and watches
over us, give His blessing to you both. Amen.'

" Ah! the few hours which remained of that
happy day flew by too quickly : it was my first happy
day in England, and my last also. Already did
misfortune hover over us; but we heard not its
stealthy approach, although a slight shuddering
foreboding oppressed my heart that my happiness
had come too suddenly upon me!

" The quiet evening had given place to the still
quieter night; numberless stars shone in the cloud-

6 THE MADMAN OF ST. JAMES'.

less sky, but the moon had not yet risen—she waited to illumine the hour of midnight.

"We stood at the window, we three happy beings; for more than two hours we had been talking of separating, but I was still there. Twice already had Bob, the old servant, brought my horse from the stable, and taken it back again; but now at last he was there again, walking Bravour up and down upon the grass before the door, looking up at us from time to time, as if he were impatient to be released from his night walk.

"More than twenty times already had I left as late as this, but never had the parting been so painful to me.

"'Stop, oh stop!' Ellinor kept on whispering softly to me. 'See,' said she, louder, 'look at the many beautiful stars, how immoveable they are, although each night they visit me; but you, my own life's star, which to-day I have discovered, you remain no longer with me.'

"'Child!' said the father, in a loving voice, 'this star will be as faithful to you as the others; even if it leaves you to-day, to-morrow it will appear to you again.'

"'To-morrow! oh yes, to-morrow! But how beautiful is to-day!'

"'And she put her arm within mine, and I felt her delicate, warm, elastic form press closer to me.'

"'The great clock now struck eleven.'

THE MADMAN OF ST. JAMES'. 7

" 'Ellinor,' said I, ' I must go! I shall not be at home before one o'clock, and at eight to-morrow morning I will be here again. I do not require rest, but you, Ellinor, you really want it.'

" 'Well, if you must go, go then! But do be here punctually at eight o'clock, my Percy.'

" I took my hat; Ellinor and her father accompanied me to the door, and went up with me to the horse, which old Bob brought to me directly.

" 'Oh, what a beautiful creature, this good Bravour is!' said Ellinor, patting with her soft hand the arched neck of the noble animal, who, gently neighing, began pawing the ground with one of his fore feet.

" 'Carry him safely home, Bravour,' said she, caressingly, to the horse, ' carry him safely; you take my life with you.'

" 'And he will bring you your life again to-morrow,' I answered, kissing her for the last time. ' Adieu!'

" I sprang into the saddle, and took hold of the bridle.

" 'Shall Othello stop here, or go with me?' I asked.

" 'Take him with you, take him with you; until the moon is up, the night is dark, and I am so anxious about you. Oh, if it were but daylight again!'

" 'But you have often let me ride this way at

8   THE MADMAN OF ST. JAMES'.

night without expressing any anxiety; and why is it not the same to-night?'

" 'No, my friend, to-night it is not the same!' said Ellinor, pressing my hand. 'But now ride slowly on, I will remain with my father at the door until we can no longer hear Bravour's steps. We shall stop here until then. Good night—good night—good night!'

" 'Good night!' I responded, and then whistled to Othello, who immediately started up joyfully, and ran on before, while I slowly followed.

" Strong and courageous as I had shown myself at parting, I felt the same painful, inexplicable anxiety as Ellinor, which, only now that I was alone, I confessed to myself. But I tried to console myself by saying to myself,—'It is the first separation that you have had to endure, you have entered into a new relation of life, unknown to you before, which exacts its dues; you will often have to feel this anxiety for your second self!'

" But, no! even this reflection did not suffice to restore my usual calmness; dark images, like shadows of an unknown world, swept over my mind; and gained at last such power over me, that, after having ridden on for more than a quarter of an hour, I turned back, saying to myself, 'You only want to see her again; it must be the mysterious impulse of a loving heart which thus influences you; and then you will return satisfied and quickly home.'

THE MADMAN OF ST. JAMES'.

" I gave the horse his head, he flew back, and immediately I felt a gentle calmness return to my heart.

" I was soon at the parsonage; but my beloved Ellinor was no longer at the door. The pale light of·a lamp showed me her chamber beneath the study of her father, who himself slept at the other side of the house; for an idea of danger never entered the minds of those who lived in this quiet part of the country. I remained a long time standing before the house, looking at it with delight. Such deep, solemn repose reigned around those lonely walls, such heavenly calmness on the lake and the wood, that, touched by the tranquillity of the scene before me, I could not sufficiently enjoy the sight 'and the feelings with which it inspired me, and remained as if fixed to the spot.

" ' No, I cannot leave it yet,' said I to myself. I rode a little way towards the wood, and fastened my horse to a young tree; then gently calling Othello to my side, who was running about among the low bushes, I said to him, ' You shall be my only companion in this beautiful night; ' and again I returned to my former post.

" Ah! this was the first time in my life that on a clear starlight night I had stood before the window of one I loved, and tried to recall her beautiful face to my mind; and I now understood, what formerly I never could, what deep poetry there is in such a night and in such a situation, and that such a sweet hour is one of the greatest enjoyments a loving heart can feel.

" 'What may she be thinking about now?' I asked myself. 'Perhaps dreaming? No; she does not sleep or dream yet, she is praying;' and I silently prayed with her. 'Can she feel that I am near her? Would she sleep quietly if she knew I was now watching beneath her window?'

" Such like sweet thoughts filled my mind; and I continued to stand there motionless and happy. And yet, when I examined my happiness, something very like a leaden weight lay upon my heart, seeming convulsively to press it down and restrain its throbs of joy. •

" I held Othello's collar with my left hand, so that he should keep quiet, and not scratch at the door, as he usually did, for admission, when suddenly I felt him slowly raise his body, and gradually and slowly stretch out his neck.

" I knew from this movement that he heard something. As I stood under the deepest shade of a large chestnut-tree, whose branches almost touched the ground, it was impossible that any one could see me, whilst I could clearly observe the whole enclosure surrounding the house before me.

" 'Hush!' said I in a low tone to Othello; and the patient and obedient animal neither moved nor made the least noise; he only stretched his tail out, as those dogs generally do when they are listening, and gave one of those peculiar sounds which they utter when they are on the scent of anything.

"But everything was perfectly quiet, not a leaf moved.—Suddenly it appeared to me as if I saw the dark outline of a man's figure among the opposite bushes; a lengthened look convinced me that I was not mistaken—it really was a man; he approached, always gently walking on the grass. He already stood opposite Ellinor's chamber-window, and trying to avoid making the least noise, he climbed up one of the nearest trees. At this moment the light in that chamber was extinguished. Soon a dark covering of leaves concealed his figure from me, and I saw nothing more of him.

"My heart beat so loudly that I could hear it, and my arm, with which I violently kept back the dog, began to tremble.

"The man now descended from the tree; slowly, gently, he sneaked, rather than walked, across the lawn towards the house, and, as far as I could see, looked about in all directions.

"At this moment a slight breeze stirred, the forerunner of the rising moon. The man now climbed —he seemed well practised in such exercise—by help of the projections of the tower to the nearest window —to Ellinor's chamber-window. Here he remained standing, looking through the window into the dark apartment within—his foot was at most only two feet from its floor.

"I could hardly breathe, but I made my preparations. Had I had my pistols by me, which were placed loaded in the saddle-pocket of my horse, I know I should have shot him, for a violent feeling of passion, such as I had never experienced before, took possession of me.

"The man put his arm up to the window, and began to feel about it for the fastening. This was the moment to act. I bent down to the ear of the dog and whispered,—

"'At him, and hold him fast!'

"I let him go; the dog flew without a sound, but swift as the wind, at his victim. It only needed a spring and a shake, and the man was on the ground; but immediately, with a quick movement, he sprang again to his feet, while Othello, in obedience to my word, contented himself with holding him fast by his clothes.

"The moon now shone forth, and I saw — ah! you know it already—I recognized Mortimer, my brother.

"'Hold!' cried he, with a suppressed cry, 'who is there?'

"And he endeavoured to shake off Othello, who had placed his great paws on his shoulders, and held him, as a panther holds his prey, only waiting for my

THE MADMAN OF ST. JAMES'.

order to begin a more serious attack upon him with his sharp teeth.

" In the passion and agitation which shook me, I began to forget that it was my own brother who stood there before me; but I still restrained myself, and said in a suppressed but firm voice,—

" ' Thief by day, and thief by night! what do you want here?'

" ' Ha!' cried he, in a low tone of rage, now only recognizing me, as the pale light of the moon had shone on his, but not on my face. ' Ha! rascal—is it you?'

" But immediately recollecting himself, he said more quietly,—

" ' Call off your dog; you surely would not wish your brother to be torn to pieces by that beast?'

" ' I wish you were not my brother,' I answered; ' then, not my dog, but I myself would be on you! Come back, Othello!—the man is too bad for you.'

" The dog obeyed, and crouched behind me, ready, however, at the first good opportunity, to spring upon him again.

" But scarcely did Mortimer feel himself relieved from the weight of the powerful animal, than his courage returned, and with it his anger.

" ' Are you here, then?' cried he, his passion bursting forth, and endeavouring to approach me. ' Do you want to get an inheritance here also?'

" ' Silence!' I cried, and do not disturb the peace

of this house with your rascally words, as with your shameless deed. You are too daring, for you are on my ground; Ellinor is affianced to me, and to-morrow, perhaps, may be my wife.'

" ' Wife?—wife? Ha! ha! Accursed wretch! *Your* wife? First be a man, and then take to yourself a wife!'

" And with these words he sprang upon me, and seized me by the throat. But keeping back Othello with my left hand, and with a call, which fortunately he obeyed, as the struggle between us was too unequal, with my right hand I powerfully grasped Mortimer by the breast of his coat, and pressed him back against a tree, endeavouring as much as possible to force him away from the house.

" I succeeded; but my opponent, rendered desperate by my success in this attempt, and still more desperate, knowing himself to be unarmed, again sprang upon me, and maliciously attempted to trip me up with his foot. But now my patience failed me; I felt that it was in my power to bring this unnatural struggle — which, although short, was violent—to an end.

" My brother was tall and powerfully formed; anger and despair redoubled his strength; but what was his strength compared to my arm of iron and broad chest—compared to me, who was so well versed in all the arts of fencing and wrestling? With the utmost calmness I parried all his blows, attacking

THE MADMAN OF ST. JAMES'.   15

him at the same time.   After some fruitless attempts
to shake him off, I took him round the waist, and
collecting all my strength, lifted him up, which least
of all he expected, and threw him like an adder
from me on the ground, so that the bushes among
which I hurled him broke and cracked underneath
him.

"Othello again attempted to rush on him, but
again I held him back.

"With a throbbing heart I stood there, not knowing what to do next; when, after a few minutes, he
rose, and throwing a stone at me, which luckily,
however, just missed my head, he shook his fist, and
gnashing his teeth, he said, with a half-suppressed
voice of scorn, as if ashamed to proclaim his defeat
aloud—

"'This time the victory is yours; but do not rejoice too soon over your success, rebellious rascal!
Not even the affianced, much less the wife, shall ever
belong to you.'

"With these words, and a deep muttered curse, he
disappeared among the shadows of the trees.

"Speechless and motionless, I stood there looking
after him, holding my faithful companion, Othello,
so that he should not rush after him and tear him to
pieces.   But my heart and limbs trembled as if
I had committed a murder, and a cold shiver ran
over me, as if I felt the approach of some great
misfortune.

THE MADMAN OF ST. JAMES'.

"How long I stood there I do not know; but slowly I recovered myself. It was not the exertion I had just had which so overpowered me; no! it was a foreboding—the foreboding of coming danger from which I could not escape—that seized upon me, and announced to me that a contest had begun which could only terminate with the death of one of us.

"But gradually I was able to reflect again calmly; my mind struggled powerfully against the sense of threatening dangers. What should I do now? Return home? Never! Ellinor's danger might perhaps not yet be over, and my assistance might again be necessary. 'Ah! she heard nothing of what has taken place,' I thought, and this was my greatest consolation; 'and she shall never know that the brother of her own betrothed would have committed such an outrage. Her repose shall not be disturbed by such disgrace, and her innocent faith in mankind be, as it were, trodden under foot!' I went back to the tree where my horse was standing, loosened saddle and bridle, so that he might lie down, and then, with Othello, took again my watch under the trees, looking up to the quiet window above, where now perhaps the sweetest dreams were hovering over the gentle Ellinor, breathing of love and hope, while under the same window brother was struggling with brother for life, and for life's dearest prize—love.

"I remained standing there until the stars faded away, until the moon disappeared, and the first warm

THE MADMAN OF ST. JAMES'. 17

rays of the rising sun gleamed over wood and field,
awakening the birds of the forest to renewed life and
joy.

"And now, saddling and mounting my horse, I
rode round the house at a little distance from it until
I saw signs of stirring in it; then I dismounted, and
knocked at the door, which was immediately opened
to me by Bob, who looked at me with astonishment,
and said—

"'What, here already, my lord? Miss Ellinor
is not yet up, but Mr. Graham is in his study reading
his prayers.'

"'I will pray with him,' I answered. 'Say nothing of my arrival, Bob, and take my horse to the
stable.'

"Throwing him the bridle, I cautiously mounted
the stairs, so that Ellinor should not hear my steps;
for the ears of love are keen.

"I tapped gently at the door, and entered. Mr.
Graham had scarcely glanced at my ruffled dress, my
excited but pale face, when he said,—

"'Good heavens, Percy! where do you come
from? What is the matter? What has happened?'

"'Nothing, sir,' I answered, in as calm a voice as
I could command—'nothing but that two brothers
have been struggling for life and death about your
honour and the honour of your daughter.'

"'Good Heavens! But no blood has been shed?'

"'No, no; for want of better weapons we two

VOL. II.   C

18   THE MADMAN OF ST. JAMES'.

athletes have been fighting only with our bare arms, and I have come off conqueror.'

"And then I related to him in what state of mind I had gone away the previous evening, and how, impelled by some foreboding of evil, I had returned, and described all that had taken place,

"'And now,' I said, in conclusion, 'you see from this, Graham, how necessary it was even yesterday to be prepared for action; you see now how your house, your lonely, unprotected house, is no longer a place of security; how even your position, as clergyman of the parish in which my father lives, is no longer respected, and that your daughter can no longer be without a powerful protector to defend her from such danger, and even to watch over her hours of rest. But one thing, Graham, I pray,' added I, hastily: 'not a word of all that has happened to Ellinor. Her repose is too precious to me to allow me to stain a thought of hers with the poison of this bad deed. You understand me. Let us two men act alone, and it shall be my task to make all our wishes and resolutions acceptable to her. I know she will act as I wish.'

"'Is it, then, come to this?' said Mr. Graham, with a face pale with fright and agitation. 'Are these my thanks for my conscientious services in the house of the marquis, and for the blameless fulfilment of the duties of my sacred calling during so many years, that his own son should dare—atrocious!

THE MADMAN OF ST. JAMES'. 19

—at night—my daughter—my only child, my darling. No, no! it is too much! But, Percy,' added Mr. Graham, with the rising fire of noble pride, 'you must permit me to act now. I must go to him—yes, I must go, to inform the doting father of the shameful conduct of his spoiled son, his honourable son! Perhaps he does not know what a treasure he possesses in him. No, he does not quite know him; but I will speak,—in Lord Mortimer's presence will I speak to him. I will take advantage of the respect he owes, as a Christian, to my calling, and as a patron to my position, and demand satisfaction for the insult which has been offered to me.'

" 'And who will be your witness, Graham,' I asked, 'that this shameful insult has been offered here? Do not hope too much. The guilty one will not confess it.'

" 'You, you, Percy, are my witness. Ah! I will —I will teach him to understand his two sons. It is now, at last, time to make him see clearly; and if one spark of religious or human feeling still glows in his cold heart, I will kindle it into a bright flame. For once I will conquer. Oh, you do not know me!'

" 'Act according to your judgment, and as you like, Graham; but in the mean time allow me also to do what I think is for the best.'

" Excited but determined, as a calm, resolute mind always is, when compelled or provoked to take a

c. 2

decided step, Mr. Graham went to put on his gown, in order to invest his undertaking with a solemnity he hoped might assist it, and I in the mean time sent Bob on a pony to Phillips, telling him to order a carriage immediately, with four horses, to be at my little house in the wood, where he himself was to await my further orders.

"By the time I had managed this, Mr. Graham, with his gown on, entered the room.

"'It is still too early,' said I to him; 'you will not be admitted.'

"'For the message of a servant of the Church, and for such an errand as mine, it is never too early. Why, lately he summoned me to him at this same hour, for his lordship has sleepless nights, and his mornings dawn sooner than ours; so let me go, go while my blood is still hot, and the matter is still fresh in my remembrance.'

"'May God give His blessing to you!' said I, taking him by the hand; 'but I have no confidence in the success of your undertaking.' For I now began to have a suspicion of the real author of all the misery which had overwhelmed us.

"He went.

"But Ellinor, the happy Ellinor, perhaps just now awaking from her peaceful slumber, thinking only of that hour which should bring her beloved again to her, perhaps even now counting the minutes until the clock should strike the wished-for hour,

THE MADMAN OF ST. JAMES'.

she did not yet know that I was already there, and that her father on her account was already on his painful journey to the castle, and that perhaps even this day might bring an event to pass, which might destroy the hope of her whole life.

"At last the clock struck eight. Then I saw her descend the stairs, go to the front door, and look out in the direction in which yesterday I had disappeared, and by which I was to return to her that day. With a joyful, elastic step she entered the wood, which was sparkling with the dew of morning. She came to the tree where Bravour had passed the night, and remained for some time before it, as if in doubt and surprise; most likely she saw the marks of the hoofs which Bravour had left behind him. Then, however, she went on her way, happy, hopeful.

"Lost in the happiness of contemplating her, I still could not forget that danger might again be near her in the wood, and with my eyes I watched every bush and path. At last Othello, who according to his usual custom had followed Bravour to the stable, now ran in search of her. I heard her joyful greeting, and then the dog's usual delighted bark of joy. 'Now,' thought I, 'she is safe;' and my thoughts again flew back to her father, whose return I awaited with impatience, for I would not see her until he had come back. But why is he so long absent?

"However, I had not to wait much longer; he returned—but how did he return? Pale, agitated,

22   THE MADMAN OF ST. JAMES'.

angry, he, usually so calm and composed! At the same moment Ellinor rushed in.

"'For Heaven's sake, what is the matter?' she cried. 'You already here, Percy, and I did not know it; and you, dear father, thus—tell me, tell me, pray, what is it? what is it?'

"'Be calm, my child!' said Mr. Graham, in a serious and trembling voice. 'Do not interfere now with our concerns; you can do no good, nay, you are even in our way; go now, and leave us to manage for you.'

"Alarmed at these words, the young girl clung to my arm. Never had she heard her father speak thus; she looked at me beseechingly.

"'Go to your room, dearest Ellinor!' I now said; 'your father is quite right; something has occurred which may have serious consequences; all this I will tell you later; but now, for my sake, dearest, go to your own room, and remain there until we come to you.'

"Ellinor went, without saying another word; she did not even cast a look back on me.

"Hardly had the door closed upon her, when Mr. Graham approached me. He had taken off his gown. Deep grief was expressed in all his features, but at the same time confidence, courage, resolution, and strength of mind. Taking both my hands in his, he said,—

"'Percy, my son, it is all over now; the trouble was all in vain.'

THE MADMAN OF ST. JAMES'.

"'Ha! all over?—all over? What did he say?'

"'Do not wish to hear what happened; suffice it to say that you, my daughter, and myself were insulted—yes, insulted. And now let us make arrangements for leaving this house and neighbourhood, which until to-day were so dear, so inexpressibly dear to me. For the future, no connection can exist between your father and myself. As poor as I came to this place do I leave it; all the money I have earned from him I will leave behind, I will return it to him.'

"I looked at him with sympathy, but inquiringly; a tear glistened in his eye, but he struggled to suppress it.

"'Yes, it is all over!' he repeated; 'do not look at me so searchingly; you must not know more, but, oh! you can imagine it. And now, answer me. Are you still willing to keep the promise you made yesterday to the now penniless and insulted clergyman's daughter—to be her adviser and protector? And are you determined to be all these to her soon?'

"'At any moment,' I answered; 'now, directly, rather than later.'

"'It is well! My blessing at least you will have; and I think, although I am only a poor clergyman, still that will be of some avail before Him to whom kings, marquises, and lords alike must pray for the fulfilment of their wishes.'

THE MADMAN OF ST. JAMES'.

" " I felt cold drops of perspiration bedew my forehead, and I trembled.

" ' Did he curse me, then?' I asked, in a low voice, almost breathless.

" ' Peace, my son! I have blessed thee; but now leave me alone for a few hours; I have some letters to write, and still much to think about. After that, I am yours—yours and Ellinor's; and if such is your wish, we will never part from each other again.'

" I now went to Ellinor. She was reasonable enough not to wish to know more than I thought fit to tell her. She resolved, yes, my friend, she resolved to become my wife that very day.

" At the end of two hours Mr. Graham joined us, and asked at what time the carriage I had ordered would be in waiting.

" ' At four o'clock this afternoon,' I answered.

" ' Very well,' said he, ' so be it! Take leave, Ellinor, of your little possessions; do not take with you more than is absolutely necessary, or particularly dear to you; leave the rest to those who gave it to us; nobody will touch it.'

" ' And when do we leave?' asked Ellinor. ' You both seem so agitated that I quite shudder to look at you. I feel that our home is no longer here; let us hasten to find another.'

" ' I think we will go directly after dinner,' said her father; ' that will be our last meal in this house.'

" At twelve o'clock Bob returned, after executing

THE MADMAN OF ST. JAMES'. 25

my orders to Phillips. In silence we partook of our meal, and then we prepared to go. Only a maidservant, who had been for some time in Mr. Graham's service, remained behind. The luggage we were to take, such as linen, clothing, &c., was placed on one pony, and Ellinor mounted the other. As I was lifting her on, she smiled on me through her tears, such a sweet smile! it was like sunshine breaking through a dark cloud.

"Bob led my horse; Mr. Graham and I went on foot, followed by Othello.

"In silence we left the place; we did not even look at each other. Each had grief to bear, and needed not that it should be increased by the sorrow of the other.

"When we had gone about three hundred steps, we all stopped, as if actuated by one and the same feeling, and turned round to look once more at that quiet sanctuary which we were leaving, which, alas! was now no longer a sanctuary for us.

"There lay that peaceful dwelling, the broad blue lake, the bright clear sky above, and our dear, quiet, green wood. We looked at each other; we pressed each other's hands, but our hearts alone expressed our feelings, our lips remained closed.

"Thus, at two o'clock in the afternoon, we left the parsonage, and it was nearly five o'clock before we reached the cottage of the forester's widow.

"Phillips was there already, waiting with the carriage and the horses."

CHAPTER II.

CONCLUSION OF THE HISTORY OF THE MADMAN OF ST. JAMES'.

HERE the relator again paused, and drew a deep breath. I did not venture to interrupt him; for, though I was waiting anxiously for what he had still to tell me, I would not rob him of a moment of his time, as daybreak could not now be far off.

He then resumed :—

"Let me quickly pass over the rest of my unhappy story, for the day will soon dawn, and it is only with effort that I trust myself to the remembrance of that which still remains for you to hear.

"About two miles from the spot where we had found and entered our carriage, at the top of a little hill grown round with trees, was a small chapel; it was in tolerable repair, and belonged formerly to an old cloister, the ruins of which excited general interest, and had been much visited on account of their architectural beauties.

"An old servant of the church, living in seclusion

from the world, had taken up his residence near this place, performing the double duty of keeping it in order, and showing it to travellers, who came to see it from far and near.

"Dimly illumined by the setting sun, that old building stood there on the hill, imparting an air of protection and peace to all around; it seemed almost as if it had been erected there for the sacred purpose which filled our hearts; for this was the spot Mr. Graham had selected at which to give me the legal and indisputable right of becoming the protector of the innocence and helplessness of his daughter.

"We entered the small sacred building with the feelings of those who, fleeing from their fellow-creatures, surrender themselves with perfect confidence to their Creator,—like those who, deprived of earthly happiness, give themselves up to that which is heavenly. Even I, who had suffered the most of the three, felt the blessed influence of its soothing calm, and forgot that mortal grief which had just before pierced my heart, and seemed to gnaw at the very root of my life.

"With these calm and peaceful feelings, I thought of my Creator with faith and perfect love; I thanked Him for the priceless gift which was to be placed at this sacred moment in my possession, and I was eager to utter that solemn vow; for firm was my determination to guard with unchanging love and devotion that beloved being at my side; and her

THE MADMAN OF ST. JAMES'.

melancholy, but still lovely, eyes seemed to promise me also her faithful love for ever !

" With the usual affecting and simple words, Mr. Graham performed that holy rite, of which only Phillips and Bob were the witnesses. Ellinor and I had pledged our irrevocable vows of unchanging love, the final blessing was pronounced by her father—by him who was the one most fitted to fill our wounded hearts with thoughts of peace,—that peace which cometh from Him who watcheth over us, and ordereth all things for our good. A silent tearful embrace, but which expressed all that was in our hearts, united us for ever. We again descended the hill, at the bottom of which our carriage waited, which we immediately entered. The postilion urged on the horses, and we travelled at full speed. I had given Phillips the charge of my horses, with directions that he should take them on, by short daily stages, to my estate at Dunsdale, where, for the present, we intended to go.

" According to his own wish, old Bob sat on the coach-box. Othello lay at our feet in the carriage; for on no account would Ellinor part with the faithful animal, who had given so many proofs of strong attachment. That Phillips was obliged to be absent was a regret for her, and for us all; for at such a time as we had just passed it is a consolation and a pleasure to have all we love around us, be it what it may.

" With the speed of the wind, we fled in the direc-

THE MADMAN OF ST. JAMES'.

tion of Dunsdale; the sun sank to rest, and the evening, with its shadows, appeared. What we spoke about, I do not now remember; but our hearts were full of the sorrows and joys of the past, refreshed, however, by the blessed feeling of safety and happiness which began gradually to take possession of us, when, suddenly, the carriage stopped, and the postilion, swearing loudly, dismounted from his horse.

"I opened one of the carriage windows, and asked what was the matter.

"'The stupid brute!' cried the postilion, once more swinging his whip, and unmercifully lashing one of the front horses. 'Often as he has done his work, he now to-day leaves me in the lurch.'

"'Do not beat him so,' said I to him; 'there is nothing else to be done than to drive to the first respectable house, and try and borrow another horse as far as the next station; or do you know any other place in the neighbourhood where we could get a good horse? We would pay well for it.'

"'Oh, yes; but that would be an hour's journey out of the way,' answered the postilion, still in a rage.

"I believed, or at least I tried to believe, that the man was acting honestly by us. I gave him a sovereign, telling him that I would not blame him for this interruption to our journey, but that he should only now exert himself to get a good horse somewhere.

"He mounted again, and, at a walking pace, we

went on for a good mile farther, when we reached at last a kind of inn; it was at some distance from the main road, and resembled more a lurking-hole for thieves than anything else.

"'You remain here,' I said to Ellinor and her father, 'and I will go and see myself about getting a horse, and try as much as I can to shorten our stay here.'

"I got out. Oh, my friend, how little did I think of what would happen to me the next moment!

"The innkeeper was in the yard, talking to some person; I found him quite willing to let me have the horse immediately, and ordered it might be harnessed.

"I was just going to return to the carriage, when, suddenly, from all parts of that dark yard, strong men rushed out upon me, and I, wholly unprepared for such an attack, was, at the first onset, thrown to the ground.

"At first I could not imagine what was happening to me, and it was only when I was again on my feet, and using all my strength with some success, that I saw the affair was taking a very serious turn.

"I already believed myself the conqueror in this strange attack, for I had shaken three or four from me, and punished them with a shower of blows, when I was struck at the back of the head by a cudgel, and once more fell to the ground.

"I now lost all consciousness, and when I regained

THE MADMAN OF ST. JAMES'. 31

it, I found myself lying in a dark carriage, the blinds of which were all drawn down. We seemed to be going at a furious rate, but in which direction I could not possibly guess, not being able to see either sky or country, even if I had had the power of moving.

"But although stunned from that violent blow on my head, I was, notwithstanding, bound hand and foot, as well as deprived of the power of speech by a handkerchief forced between my teeth,—thus rendered doubly unable to make the least effort to extricate myself from such a humiliating position, even if I had had the strength left in me to do so.

"In the carriage were seated three men whom I did not know; they looked at me stupidly and in silence when I opened my eyes; and from time to time one of them wiped off the warm drops of blood which trickled down my face from the wound in my head.

"Had I even been able to speak at this moment, I should certainly have remained speechless; for anger, rage, despair, enough to deprive any human being of his senses, made me dumb, and hardly allowed me, when I had the power of reflection, to think calmly of the fearful change which had suddenly transformed me, after only a taste of happiness, into one of the most miserable of mortals.

"How long we journeyed on over hill and valley without stopping I do not know; for from time to time I lost again all consciousness; and when at length I fully recovered, I found myself—sir, can you not guess it?—at the place—here—where you have found me.

"The half-raving, half-stunned state in which I arrived at St. James' must have continued for some length of time, for at first I could remember only with difficulty the different events which had taken place.

"But one morning, on awakening from a restless sleep, during which the most dreadful dreams had tormented me, I found myself in a quiet room, in which I remarked four men, my keepers, and several instruments, the use and purpose of which were then unknown to me.

"I asked for something to drink; it was given to me; but, as it appeared to me, not without some misgiving, lest I should throw the tin mug, in which I had received it, into the face of the man who had handed it to me.

"At the usual hour—it was towards evening—the doctors came in. I half awoke, but I did not open my eyes, for I wanted to hear what they would say about my state.

"They had, however, only uttered a few words, when I found out where I was.

"'What!' cried I, in a voice which seemed to terrify all those present, 'In a madhouse have they confined me? Do they think I am mad?'

THE MADMAN OF ST. JAMES'. 33

"And with these words I tried to rise; but now remarked, for the first time, that I was secured to the bed by means of a broad strap. But before any one could prevent me, I had collected all my strength, burst the bonds which bound me against all moral and human right, and with one spring I was out of bed.

"They rushed upon me; once more a fearful struggle ensued; three of the keepers were already stretched on the floor, when the doctors, who had rushed out, now appeared with assistance.

"A large blanket was cleverly thrown over my head; in this manner I was thrown on the floor, and, amid oaths and curses, bound hand and foot with the already mentioned instruments.

"I was then placed under an icy-cold shower-bath, which at first nearly deprived me of my consciousness; but still it was of use to me, for I became quiet and thoughtful.

"And shall I tell you what feeling this dreadful power of thought called forth in me? No, you are a doctor, but you are a human being as well. You know about it; but these dreadful feelings, crippling both mind and body, urged me to fresh paroxysms of rage and despair. Gradually I began to see clearly that violence was of no use to me, even if I intimidated my tormentors; and I, therefore, called reason to my aid, which I might so easily have lost for ever under such circumstances, and resolved to bear

VOL. II.   D

34   THE MADMAN OF ST. JAMES'.

with manly fortitude all that at present I had to endure.

"But it was a long time before any one trusted me; notwithstanding my resolutions, there were often moments when, tormented with sorrows and heart-breaking recollections of the past, I again did what I ought not to have done, and was sometimes so angry and enraged at the rudeness which, in defiance of the strict orders of the superintendent, some of my keepers showed towards me, that I felt compelled to punish them myself for it; but, after such vain attempts to help myself, I always got the worst of it; force was always called in to subdue me, and they, you know, had a thousand arms at command, while I had but two.

"Thus six long months passed away; they now began to act more gently towards me, and to place some confidence in me, most likely more for the sake of proving me—which at that time, however, I never suspected—than because they were certain of any obedience or amendment on my part.

During this period of gentle treatment, the thought awoke in me of the possibility of being able to regain my lost liberty; this idea cheered and strengthened me, and I began to recover myself.

" I now formed plans for that purpose, and determined, by a well-contrived escape, to elude the vigilance of my guards. But though I acted with the greatest precaution and reflection on a settled plan, all was in vain; my intention was discovered and baffled; for they understood how to act with precaution and reflection, and could form plans just as well as I did. In a word, all my various attempts later too were fruitless; and I thereby, as you yourself have seen, have only drawn upon myself the more the notice and watchfulness of the officers and their assistants.

"Then, for the sake of having something useful to do, I devoted myself to the benefit of several of the patients, speaking to them kindly and reasonably, after I had once obtained their confidence. I assured them of my good-will, and this assurance I found was very important. I thus obtained friends, if you like to call them so; for I was successful in most of my friendly attempts. A single word from me was often sufficient with a lunatic to effect that which all the threats and violence of the keepers could not bring about; and I thus learnt to perceive that a gentle, although serious and persuasive mode of treatment towards such patients is productive of the best and quickest results.

"I often spoke to the officials on this subject; they were good-natured enough to listen to me, although I never remarked that they acted on my word, for how could any clever suggestion come out of such a crazed head as mine?

"But I found that these conversations had an influence on the treatment of the doctors towards my-

36 THE MADMAN OF ST. JAMES'.

self. I got better food, and obtained generally what
I asked for; they gradually even became obliging
and friendly towards me, and I began, for one in a
madhouse, to lead an endurable life; I was allowed
to read, to walk when I liked, to work, to tire myself, and then to rest, as I felt disposed. My sleep
became undisturbed and more refreshing; I felt
myself restored to my usual health and strength.

" At last the idea occurred to me to confide in the
director, who almost daily conversed with me. I
tried it—he smiled. Ah! that smile told me that he
knew it all better than I did. They listened to me;
I was allowed to write to my father under another
address;—he had taken care not to let his real name
be known, and I also was known only by the name
I bear here;—and I wrote to my father, for I did not
think at that time that he had any share in the vil-
lanous deed which had brought me here. I attri-
buted all that had happened to the hatred, jealousy,
and revenge of my brother.

" My letter was sent. The director received the
reply; but it was a reply which destroyed all my
hopes, and made my blood run cold in my veins; for
my father, my own father, declared me to be perfectly mad, and accused me of conduct towards himself and my brother which, related to a stranger
unacquainted with all that had passed, might certainly
have rendered me liable to the suspicion of the most
undoubted insanity.

THE MADMAN OF ST. JAMES'. 37

"My heart, my strong manly heart, now sank; and I determined for the present to be calm, and to bear with patience what I could not change, trusting in a merciful God to decide how long I was to bear these trials, and in what way it should please Him to end them.

"Thus two years passed away!"

"And Ellinor and Mr. Graham?" I interrupted him, unable any longer to refrain from asking this question.

"Yes! where they are?—where they are? You shall hear directly. Two years, I say, passed thus, when one day, walking in the park, watched by the usual attendants, I saw—imagine my joy and surprise—I suddenly saw Phillips, my good, faithful Phillips, coming towards me, dressed in the way you have seen him.

"I was almost stunned by this joyful unexpected sight—I felt a convulsive feeling of delight in my heart and mind which exercises its beneficial influence over me to this day.

"I endeavoured to appear calm, and so did Phillips, for he gave me a furtive look, which cautioned me not to recognise him. The good man himself turned quite pale on seeing me suddenly standing before him; he turned round as if looking anxiously for something; then he observed me from a distance with such emotion visible on his manly face, that I could see it was with difficulty he repressed the tears

38   THE MADMAN OF ST. JAMES'.

which filled his eyes. This faithful, noble-hearted
man had made it the business of his life, just as he is
at this moment devoting himself to discover Ellinor's
place of abode—to find out mine; but all his efforts
for two years had been in vain.

"The better to be able to arrive at his purpose,
and to make his appearance here and in other places
less a subject for observation, he had taken up the
trade of a travelling pedlar. He came into this
neighbourhood without any distinct hope; he had
heard of the Madman of St. James', for by this name
—I know not why—I soon came to be called by the
whole neighbourhood; but he never had the least
idea that in the lunatic, who excited such general
sympathy, he should find—me!

"Never in my life shall I forget the blessed but
most melancholy feeling which came over me after
the first surprise. The past and the remembrance
of its beautiful bright moments awoke afresh in my
almost frozen heart; life once more obtained the
charm of hope, and I looked forward again to the
future.

"Phillips had contrived to obtain permission from
the director to furnish several of the wealthy patients
with articles of convenience and amusement;—he
thus found the opportunity of speaking with me.

"Ah! how sweet did the tone of his voice sound to
my ear; how did it touch my heart, which so long had
thirsted after friendship, confidence, and kindness.

THE MADMAN OF ST. JAMES'. 39

"We both related to each other all that had happened since we parted—and while appearing only to be showing me his wares, and telling me their prices, he told me all he had to say.

"According to my orders, he had ridden on slowly towards Dunsdale Castle, and arrived there on the evening of the third day. He had of course not found me there, and, worse still, neither Ellinor nor her father. Our non-arrival was inexplicable; he became uneasy; two days—a week—a fortnight—passed; he waited. At last, unable to bear this state of suspense any longer, he returned to the place where he had left us, but nobody knew anything about us, or could in the least dispel his anxiety.

"Now he began to suspect some foul play; he sent out private messengers in all directions, and secretly and with the greatest caution tried to make inquiries in my father's house. One night he returned to his sister and to the deserted parsonage; but nowhere could he see or learn the least clue to us.

"He then set forth on a pilgrimage of fruitless search, and never did a nobler or more faithful heart undertake it. The two years had been for him as melancholy as for me, until a good Providence had thus led him to St. James'.

"His and my wishes were thus far fulfilled, and we kept up a constant communication with each other. He came as frequently as he could, and we began anew plans for escape. Up to this time, however, all have proved unsuccessful, until, a short time ago, the idea occurred to him of getting his present little basket waggon, on which our hopes rested with greater confidence.

" But I have still got a few words to tell you about the last two years I have spent here. I obtained permission of the directors to have a horse; for, according to the written instructions sent on my entrance into St. James', I was to receive all the comforts suitable to my means and habits, so that they might not appear to act too villanously towards me.

" Phillips brought me my own horse—my Bravour. Ah! I cannot describe to you what I felt when for the first time I again mounted him; when he, who had so often borne me to my Ellinor, was now with me—in a madhouse!

" I then removed to the apartments I now occupy, and gradually filled them with all the articles which Phillips pretended to sell me; and it was only when my resolution of being gentle was blotted out by the fearful mental distress and anxiety I could not forget, and the indignities I had suffered, that I had again some paroxysms of scorn and rage, the treatment for which is known to you.

" These attacks, however, became more rare, and by degrees the watch over me became less strict; and I began, partly by presents and partly by

THE MADMAN OF ST. JAMES'. 41

kind words, to win over some of the keepers, who, as much as they possibly could, sought to lighten the misery of my life here. But since your arrival, I know not for what reason, the general vigilance has again increased, as if they had now an indistinct notion that I am working harder and am more determined than ever to effect my escape.

" Phillips had not omitted in his many wanderings to search just as anxiously for Ellinor and her father as for me; but all these endeavours were in vain.

" About six weeks ago, however, he discovered some clue, which appeared to him to be the right one. He was mistaken, as you know; but that at the same time he had discovered some trace of my brother, who was also in pursuit of Ellinor, you did not know until now. At present he is engaged in the same search.

" Finally, I did not omit through him secretly to make one more attempt to communicate with my father; but this last effort was just as unsuccessful as were the others. The director again received the reply, which contained the same instructions—that they should continue to watch over me with the greatest severity, and by every possible means strive to restore me to my senses, so that, when I had perfectly recovered, at the end of a few years, I might be discharged, and not cause my family so much anxiety and sorrow as I had done until now by my dreadful state of madness.

THE MADMAN OF ST. JAMES'.

" Thus, my friend," concluded the relator, " have I come to the end of my unhappy story. It was only when I saw you here that a new life seemed to open to me. By your looks I could understand you; I could see that you possess feelings in common with me, which no one here seems to have—a warm, feeling heart; and the idea which has long been in my mind, has sprung up again there with fresh hope —to escape, and this escape I can only manage with the help of one living in the house, and who is acquainted with all connected with it."

" Escape?" I asked.

" Yes!"

" And then?"

" Ask no more! You will have wondered at the forbearance with which I have spoken to you of my father and brother; this forbearance is now at an end. For four long years to be confined and treated as a lunatic! These years have made me forget that I have any duties to perform towards this father and brother; all the anger and fury which I have so long restrained I can control no longer; and I burn, so soon as I shall have escaped from this imprisonment, to *revenge* myself in a manner which shall be severe, but just also. But before I raise my hand in any way against him who has brought dishonour upon me, I must have found my Ellinor; she and her father are the only living witnesses against those who wished, by such dreadful means, not only to have robbed me

of life, but of life's best and choicest blessings—
liberty and reason."

I was going to ask him another question, when I
thought I heard a door above us violently closed.

"Hush!" said I, "what was that?"

We both listened in silence. For some time past
I fancied I had heard some movement in the passages,
and in the rooms above us. Day was already
breaking, but it was certainly still too early for the
noise of general stirring, which seemed to be taking
place in the wards of the patients in the upper rooms.

"Do you hear, sir?" I asked.

"Yes! I hear some persons walking about, and
now some one speaking."

Again all was still—then we could distinctly hear
a door open and shut, then another, then several.

"What do you think of it?" asked my companion, after listening anxiously to these several
noises.

"I am much afraid, my lord, that something has
been discovered respecting you."

"Not yet," he answered, only now drinking the
glass of wine I had placed before him when first he
came, although years most likely had passed since he
had tasted any thing of the kind.

"You had better go into my bedroom," said I.
"I will open the door and see what it is."

He immediately followed my advice. It became
lighter and lighter. I now listened attentively once

THE MADMAN OF ST. JAMES'.

more at the door before opening it. Several persons with rapid steps seemed to be going up and down stairs—all appeared to be in the greatest hurry. The suspicion, which from the first moment had seized me, became stronger. I slowly unlocked the door, opened it a little way, and put my head out: I thought perhaps I might hear some one speak. I involuntarily started, for just at this moment Mr. Lorenz had passed my door. Happily he had already passed, and thus could not have remarked this circumstance. But he had not advanced many steps when, hearing the noise I had made with my door, he turned round.

I had quickly recovered myself, and went out into the corridor to him. He came up to me, and, as it seemed to me, looked at me in a very perplexed manner.

" What is the matter, sir ? " I asked. " I hear such an unusual noise so early."

" Deuce take it ! " he answered. " Why, have you not heard it, eh ? He is gone, our madman, Mr. Sidney—that good, reasonable Mr. Sidney."

" What," I cried, with affected surprise, " has he got away ? "

" Escaped, escaped ! Yes, yes ; but come now, you can help us to look for him ; you know all his favourite haunts, if he is still any where about here."

" Just excuse me, sir, for a moment," I replied. " I shall not be long dressing."

" Well, be quick ! "

THE MADMAN OF ST. JAMES'. 45

Although I was still dressed in my usual clothes, I just made this excuse for going into my bedroom to tell my friend what was going on.

On entering, I found him slowly walking up and down the room, wiping his forehead with his pocket-handkerchief.

"They are indeed looking for you," I said to him quickly in a low voice. "I will go out and leave the door open."

"But you surely are not suspected?" asked he.

"I should think not; otherwise Mr. Lorenz would not have passed my door without speaking."

"That is right—that is all right then. Only make haste and go, I will find means to get out."

I quickly put on another coat, pressed my poor friend's hand, and ran after Mr. Lorenz, whom I found engaged very busily in searching all the rooms of the second story.

The absence of the patient from his room had been discovered in a very simple manner by Mr. Derby. He had been called up towards morning to somebody taken seriously ill in a room in the upper story; on his return, as in the mean time it had become quite light, he had remarked the door of the well-known room standing open, as Mr. Sidney, on account of the noise it would make, did not shut his door on coming to me. Mr. Derby had entered, gone into his bed-chamber, touched the bed, and found no one there. He had then immediately

46 THE MADMAN OF ST. JAMES'.

roused the porter, who had fallen asleep, but, unable to obtain from him any information about the matter, he had hastened to Mr. Lorenz and to the director, and thus the whole house was set in motion.

In the hurry of searching and making inquiries, they had forgotten to sound the alarm-bell, which would give the keepers and watchmen outside the walls notice that a patient had escaped. It was only after I had been for some time actively engaged in the search with Mr. Lorenz, that the bell rang, and its hurried and vibrating tones were loud enough to be heard a mile distant round the neighbourhood.

"And is he not yet found?" I asked of the director as he approached us, for I was not quite free from a feeling of anxiety that he might be suspected of being in my room, where search might be made and the lost one found to my great discomfiture. To have a bad conscience in a matter which touches one's honour is always a very disagreeable affair.

However, I soon discovered that no suspicion attached to me; especially as I appeared to be as eager as any of the others to find him.

All the servants were stirring; every room and corridor was searched; they shouted and called, some even ran about the park; every one was active; and I could see distinctly how much importance was attached to the safe custody of this patient so mysteriously confided to them, and now supposed to have effected his escape. It seemed as if a state prisoner had disappeared, rather than as if a lunatic had got out of a madhouse.

When our search in the house was over, and we were just going into the park, where most of the others had assembled, we had again to pass by my door. It stood wide open—I looked anxiously in. Mr. Lorenz stopped and said,—

"Ah, sir, have you some water in your room? I should like some, I am so extremely thirsty."

The bottle of wine and the *two* glasses on my table now occurred to me : in imagination I already saw my bedroom door opened, and him who was concealed there seized. But how great was my astonishment, and my relief also, in seeing only *one* wine-glass there, and that empty, although I had left it full, the bottle corked upon the table, and nothing betraying the presence of any recent visitor.

The doctor, who had immediately entered the room with me, poured out a glass of water—a jug of water also stood upon the table—and drank it ; but appeared to be all the time carefully examining everything he saw. He replaced the glass on the table, and was just going, when he said,—

"Oh ! I beg your pardon, will you allow me to enter your bedroom?" and saying these words he advanced to the door. Happily he could not see my pale face and its alarmed and agonised expression, which I saw myself but all too well reflected in the glass. He was just on the point of opening the door, when the director, passing along the corridor, called loudly for Mr. Lorenz.

He immediately obeyed this call, and hurried out with me. The director exchanged some words with him, and we again went down stairs into the garden. There, suddenly turning to me, he said, in a peculiar voice, as if he attached some importance to the question, at least so it seemed to my bad conscience, although it might have been really quite natural,—

" Did you have any visitors last evening?"

" Yes," answered I, carelessly, " Mr. Broomfield was there." And these words were quite true; for in my absence the chaplain had really been a few minutes in my room, and nearly emptied a bottle of wine which happened to be on the table.

" Well, then, I am astonished," continued Mr. Lorenz, " that he did not quite empty it, for it is not his usual custom to stop half-way in such an undertaking."

" He really seems to have some suspicion," said I to myself; but I was mistaken; a fact, however, which I did not find out for a long time afterwards.

We now entered the park. Every moment some messenger arrived to say that the runaway was not yet found.

We went down several paths, and were turning into a thick shrubbery, when, to our astonishment,

THE MADMAN OF ST. JAMES'. 49

with slow steps advanced towards us the lost one, his hands folded behind him as usual, and seemingly buried in the deepest thought.

I glanced quickly at his face: it was still somewhat flushed. To me his eyes still spoke the eloquent language of the sorrow, excitement, and pain he had lately undergone; but otherwise his features wore their usual expression of calmness, as he looked up at us inquiringly.

"Ha! there you are, Mr. Sidney!" exclaimed the director and Mr. Lorenz at the same time; "where were you? For more than an hour and a half have we all been looking for you."

"I am in the park, as you see," was the simple answer.

"And how is it that you are in the park thus early, if I may be allowed to ask?" continued the director.

"From caprice, if you like it, sir; or from necessity, if you like that better. I had slept long enough, and my room was so warm that I longed to breathe the fresh air—and so here I am."

Even this innocent, and certainly in his case necessary, falsehood, I noticed he uttered with difficulty; and Mr. Lorenz, who was a pretty keen observer, looked at him rather doubtfully.

"And who left your room door open?" resumed Mr. Elliotson.

"That is not my affair, sir, but most probably the man who did not close it."

VOL. II.   E

THE MADMAN OF ST. JAMES'.

" That sounds pretty well. Ha, ha! Morton," said he, turning to one of the keepers standing near us, "send the porter and the man who had the charge of Mr. Sidney last night to my room immediately. Who was the man?"

" Mr. Chappert," answered, half aloud, one of the bystanders.

" Aha!" said the director, "I will discharge the rascal for his carelessness; and you, Mr. Sidney, do you also retire to your room. I shall speak with your doctors concerning you; you are either more ill than you yourself imagine, or have too many whims and caprices."

And thus speaking, he retired, accompanied by the others. Slowly, and surrounded by several keepers, followed the Madman of St. James'—for such he still was in all eyes but mine—but he smiled when I turned round to look after him, observing with seeming indifference the flight of a crow, which, starting up before us, flew over the boundaries of the madhouse, and then disappeared in the misty distance.

CHAPTER III.

PLANS FOR A BOLD UNDERTAKING.

In the course of this day, which had begun so confusedly for me, I had only an opportunity of speaking five minutes with the Viscount of Dunsdale, and this was in the park during the time for general exercise. During the remainder of the day I could not possibly manage to get near him, for—"for his caprice, or from necessity, if he liked it better," as Mr. Elliotson had repeated—the usual punishment of confinement to his room had been imposed. During our brief meeting, not a word had passed respecting his own situation; but he was chiefly occupied with the anxious position the good-natured Chappert had been placed in by his fault. He gave me the necessary instructions as to what I should do for the poor man, and when I took leave of him, he placed a folded paper in my hand.

On leaving Mr. Sidney, I proceeded to visit Chappert, whom I found in his room, low-spirited and anxious; for the director had not only given him a severe reprimand, but had announced to him his speedy dismissal. On my entrance, he immediately got up, and came towards me.

"Chappert," said I to him, "You did somebody a service last night, which I hear has brought you into trouble."

"Eh! the deuce, sir! what did Mr. Sidney want to leave his room for? I have been punished enough for my good nature!"

"Yes, Chappert, and he who has been the occasion of it, is truly sorry for it."

"That is no affair of his, sir; I love the man, and would perhaps have done still more for him if he had required it."

"Well, he asks nothing more now of you for himself; on the contrary, he has sent me here for your sake, under, however, a solemn promise on your part that you will say nothing about the reason of my coming."

"Ah, sir! why should I? I have got my secrets, also, which nobody shall ever know."

"Well, for the inconvenience you have experienced for your good nature, Mr. Sidney sends you this trifle." And with these words I handed him a ten-pound note, which I had received for him.

"What can you think of me, sir?" asked Chappert, angrily. "Ten pounds for such a trifle? No, no, sir! I want nothing. If I do anybody a service, I do it for my own pleasure, and because I have my own particular reasons for so doing; but never

THE MADMAN OF ST. JAMES'. 53

for the sake of money. That is both against my duty and my conscience."

"Good!" said I, replacing the bank-note in my pocket-book. "If you do not want the money now, I will take care of it for you. And in the second place, I have got something else to propose to you, and that you will not refuse me, I hope."

"What is it?" said the man, with an anxious look. "Has this got anything to do with Mr. Sidney, also?"

"To do with him? Yes! If I am not mistaken, you have a wife and children."

"Yes! that I have—and thank God for it! Yes!"

"Then it must be painful for you to lose your situation?"

"Why, you see, sir, I don't think it will come to that yet; the director does not discharge a man who is useful so easily; they cannot find others so quickly. And if I am sent away—well, I am heartily tired of my place."

"I am glad to hear that, for your own sake; but in case you should lose your situation, I have got a proposal to make to you."

"Well, sir, what is it?"

"In case, then, that you should be obliged to leave your present situation, and are not able to find another, I have in my hands instructions to a lawyer in London, that some provision may be made for you, which I am ready to give into your possession as soon as you shall have left this house. Should I, however, leave this house before you do, you shall receive the necessary papers at my departure. In case, however, that you should be inclined to take another situation, I have still the power of proposing this to you, in case certain things change—and—they will change too ——"

"Stop, sir! With this Mr. Sidney, you mean—the Madman of St. James'?"

"Do not ask any questions," I said; "for I am not at liberty to answer them."

"All right, sir; I understand. But if you will not tell about it, at least you will allow me to make a remark upon this—this extraordinary gentleman, as we are talking about him, and are alone?"

"And what have you got to say?" asked I, curious to know more; for the man, while thus speaking, appeared to be regarding me with an extremely intelligent look.

"You will most likely smile," continued he, "that I should have an opinion on this point; but it does not signify. *I have one*, just as much as those gentlemen, the doctors, have theirs."

"Well, well, speak; you make me curious."

"Now, then, out with it. Do you really believe, sir, that this man, whom they call here the Madman of St. James'—just as if he, among them all, were the only mad one—that he, I say, is really mad?"

I looked at the man with astonishment, for he said

THE MADMAN OF ST. JAMES'. 55

this in the most good-natured and convinced manner possible.

" Yes, yes !" he continued, " I see you are astonished; but *I* think now that he is the least mad of any of them."

" And what justifies such an opinion on your part ?"

" Ah ! sir, that is difficult to be explained. I am no theoretician, as the gentlemen say; but for so many years I have had to do with lunatics, that I have acquired some practical knowledge on that point."

I was at first, indeed, astonished at this extraordinary and unexpected conversation; but, in point of fact, I need not have been much surprised at it. For how often do we find that those in the lowest class of life display, in many circumstances, much more correct judgment than those far their superiors in education and learning ! Their judgment does not rest upon reasons—at least, not on reasons of which they themselves are aware—it appears rather to be an instinctive impulse which leads them to a knowledge of that which is right, especially if, as was here the case, experience also comes into play. Let the man have acquired his knowledge where and how he might, I was pleased, nay, delighted, with his remark, and, pressing his hand, I said,—

" Keep to yourself what you have just expressed to me. I, at least, shall not forget your words, and the future alone can prove whether or not you are right."

"But what do *you* think?" he inquired, with a cunning look.

"Nothing!" I answered. "You perform your duty, and keep firm to your good opinion of Mr. Sidney."

"Aha, sir! we understand each other; and—there is my word as an honest man upon it—I will keep firm to my good opinion of him, and hope some day to be able to prove it to him. I have still to thank him for his kind wish to reward me, and please, sir, will you tell him so?"

"I will. Good day!"

"Good day, sir!"

I left him, and was now at last, for the first time, alone, and able to think quietly over the communications which had been made to me during the preceding night. This fearful wickedness exercised, to make it worse, by a father against his son, and a brother against a brother, was revolting to my feelings, and vied with all I had ever imagined of abominable, unprincipled wickedness.

Thus, between me and this unfortunate being, who, from the first hour of our acquaintance, had awakened such deep sympathy in me, there was no longer any secret. The mystery was unveiled; the sympathy which drew me towards him was explained; the dark foreboding which shadowed my spirit was

THE MADMAN OF ST. JAMES'. 57

made clear; the boundary of reserve was overstepped :
I was no more a stranger to him. I was the only
one in this great house who, besides Chappert,
rightly understood him. I was initiated into all the
sorrows of his life. Yes, sorrow quickly binds together souls who understand each other. This I felt
now more than ever, and I made a steadfast resolution that not in vain should he have chosen me
among so many. I would prove to him that I was
worthy of his confidence; that I was a man, and had
a feeling heart, such as he had yearned for so long,
and now needed more than ever.

I went over again, mentally, the chief events of
his sad history. The more I reflected, the greater
was my desire to have this fearful drama ended in
favour of him who played therein the principal
part; the more anxious I became to put a hand to
the work, and, if it were but possible, to free him
from captivity, and reinstate him in all his possessions.

Thus it was that, in the warmth and earnestness of
my feelings, I made and then rejected all kinds of
plans, until, at last, one idea remained fixed in my
mind, which, if Percy had no objection, I resolved to
put into execution as soon as possible.

Suddenly all my youthful love of adventure awoke
in me again. I beheld myself in the midst of a complete labyrinth of human wickedness. What, then,
could be more exhilarating and delightful to any one,

loving danger and excitement as I did, than to break those bonds which had bound him, against all right and justice; to restore peace and order, where violence and crime had tyrannically torn asunder all the ties of nature, and had trodden them under foot?

Later, however, in calmer moments, such as will come over us when we allow the occurrences of the day to pass quietly in review before us, I formed a more feasible plan. I thought of stating my opinion of the case to the director himself, to make him the confidant of our secret, and thus to render it even his duty to co-operate with us in liberating him who had been, in such a shameful manner, treacherously given to his charge.

Which of my two plans was to be adopted I naturally wished, and, of course, was obliged, to leave to him, who alone ought to decide. I, for my part, was ready to act on either; I was ready to execute any of his wishes; and, if the one was unsuccessful, I should, without hesitation, adopt the other, if even a forced flight from the asylum should prove to be our last alternative.

In the last case, however, I must go more cautiously to work; for there was a consideration connected with this which was sacred to me, and which I wished to touch as little as possible. This was the connection in which I stood to the director, less than to the doctors of the establishment. Mr. Elliotson had received and treated me with hospitality : I could not be ungrateful to him. I considered, however, that this flight was most likely unavoidable, and soon saw that Chappert could be of the greatest service to us. I determined, therefore, not to lose sight of this man,—who, just as he himself expected, was pardoned by his employer, and reinstated in his former situation,—and I resolved to ascertain fully, from time to time, his views and opinions with respect to my friend.

As I had no other object here than to rescue an innocent victim from the hands of violence and fraud, my conscience readily sanctioned these inquiries. I felt justified in making them, and, brought before the highest tribunal of justice, I could defend them conscientiously, with all the strength of my heart and its convictions.

But before we could determine on any particular mode of action of any description, we must first await the return of the pedlar Phillips; for he it was who knew, better than any one else, all the circumstances necessary for us to know of what occurred outside the walls of the madhouse.

Perhaps he might know the present abode of the Marquis of Seymour ; it was even not impossible that during his last journey he might have learned something important, and for his master something above price—news of Ellinor and her father.

The conversation I had on all these subjects with

Mr. Sidney took place the next day in the park during the drilling exercises, when we contrived to steal away for a few moments from the overseers, to enlighten each other upon at least some of the leading points; but upon the second evening after this day, we succeeded in conversing freely; for the period of his arrest had expired, and permission had been granted him to walk for an hour, accompanied by his usual attendants, among whom this time was Chappert; and it was he who, passing through the billiard-room, where I happened to be by accident, came to me and said,—

"Mr. Sidney begs for your company in the park, sir. He may walk again now. You will meet him near the great bench."

"Ah, my lord," said I, in a low voice, when I was quite near him—but he immediately interrupted me, and said, gently touching my arm,—

"Friend of my heart—the only confidant of my soul—never, wherever we are, wound me by addressing me thus; for you I am only Percy, or—you understand—Sidney."

"I understand. Well, if you like it better, then, Percy ——"

"Say rather Sidney, Sidney; you might perhaps compromise yourself."

"Good! Well, Mr. Sidney, how happy I am at last, without interruption, to be able to exchange a serious word with you. It is not necessary that I

THE MADMAN OF ST. JAMES'. 61

give you the assurance of my unchanging friendship."

"Ah, let that be; I believe you without words. We have just now more important matters to speak of. What were you going to say?"

"Ah! I have much upon my heart for you."

"And I for you also," he replied. "I have not been idle; and if we only act in future as much as we plan and think now, and carry only the half into execution, we may be well satisfied with ourselves. But speak quickly, for the time is short; what have you got to tell me first?"

"My first proposal is this," said I, "to take the director into our confidence, and thus perhaps to accomplish by kindness ——"

"Nothing, nothing of the kind," interrupted he almost violently; "no confidence and no confidant— least of all any one here. My patience is exhausted; at last I must act. That they should be convinced, is not to be expected; and even if you ever did succeed in convincing them, it would be too late, much too late. Never forget that for four, four long years, I have been confined and treated as a lunatic, and that as soon as I have regained my freedom, I shall use all the powers of mind and body with which nature has gifted me to pay back and be revenged on those who have been the cause of the sufferings I have endured, and the degradation which can never be entirely effaced. I have become cautious and careful from

62   THE MADMAN OF ST. JAMES'.

necessity, and for the future shall find ways and means to protect myself against all treachery and deceit. Spare yourself, therefore, all this unnecessary trouble of trying to convince these gentlemen. And if—if this did not succeed, what do you think would become of you?"

"By Jove! why, they would not shut me up, and put me under a shower-bath, would they?"

"No, perhaps not that, but they would give you a respectable escort, a kind wish for a good journey, and see you safely off the premises. Depend on it, they would make but short work of it; and you would not be the first rebel against their rules whom they have managed to get rid of quietly. For me, it would be then all the worse. Besides, it is my most earnest wish that no one else should be acquainted with my affair. The secret does not concern me alone; it is an unhappy family secret, which, much as it may be lamented, must not be made public."

"I am quite ready to act according to your wishes," I answered; "but I thought I would tell you all the plans I had to propose."

"And I am quite contented to hear them. They may be of use to us; for while speaking of all these, it will become clearer to us what we *ought* to do, and what we ought *not* to do, in order to attain our object. What else have you to propose?"

"Before you began your history, you asked me to become the judge of you and of your future actions.

THE MADMAN OF ST. JAMES'. 63

I find you are determined to revenge yourself like a man for the shame they have put upon you, and in this I perfectly agree with you, for you have the whole world and its favourable opinion on your side; and there will be found enough right-minded judges in England who will take a pleasure in deciding the case in your favour, provided you are declared sane, and can be considered no longer as Mr. Sidney of St. James', but as Viscount Dunsdale. But before you reflect on the speediest accomplishment of your wishes—before you think of the difficulties attending an escape from St. James'—there is, in my opinion, one other method of making this flight unnecessary, and also of gaining possession of the rights usurped by others. Your departure from this asylum would, in this way, be a legal one, if even the authorities here considered you as the cured Mr. Sidney, rather than the unlawfully and erroneously detained Viscount Dunsdale."

"Ah! I am curious about this, which, in one point of view, is an excellent method. I also, I must confess it frankly, have thought of such a plan as this; but I hardly dared to name it to you."

"And why should you not dare?"

"Because the entire trouble of its accomplishment would fall on you alone; for you alone could take this path of kindness, and rescue me from violence, and my unhappy secret from publicity."

"Well, if that is all," answered I joyfully, "tell

me all quickly; I begin to think the plans we have thought of are very much alike, and with respect to my readiness to act on them, be assured that I consider the whole affair not so much yours as mine, and will, therefore, fear no danger or trouble where I can be of any service to you."

"Then in nothing have I been mistaken in you, my beloved friend; receive my warmest thanks for your love. You have removed a heavy weight from my heart. Hear now my well-considered plan, and if even you accuse me of contradiction, perhaps even of unmanliness—for the judgments of the world are often hard and cruel—I cannot help it; my heart, although indignant and deeply wounded, is not made of iron or stone. No, I cannot forget that the man who has so degraded and insulted me, who has almost destroyed me, is my father. If there was only a possibility of bringing him to see how unnaturally he has acted towards me, and of letting him make all good again, well, then, indeed, all might end peaceably without the exposure of legal proceedings. I fear this possibility is very improbable, but the attempt must be made; and, as you have permitted me, you must know that I have looked to you for making this improbable impossibility possible, and even probable."

He looked at me inquiringly, with his large expressive eyes. I only nodded, smiled, and said, "Well, then, by different paths we have arrived at

THE MADMAN OF ST. JAMES'. 65

the same object, though I do not deserve your praise. Good will alone is all I possess; the rest many others share with me. But continue."

"My dearest friend! Go then to my father; act then according to your judgment, conviction, and power. I will give you leave to try everything which you may consider desirable and important. May the blessing of God attend you on your wearisome and dangerous journey, and take the blessed conviction with you that you have wished to perform the noblest action that a Christian can perform—that of reconciling a father and son who, unhappily, are at variance, and of rendering unnecessary the interference of law and unnatural violence. But how will you manage to leave St. James' when you have openly declared your intention of remaining here some time longer?"

"Let me manage that matter; I have already thought about it. In London I have a friend of some celebrity, the friend also and former fellow-student of my father, the celebrated Sir John ——; I have already visited him twice, and shall do so again before I leave England. To him I am now going to write, to beg he will recall me from this place on the plea of urgent business, under the promise, however, of soon being able to return here again. The explanation of this extraordinary request I shall promise to give him verbally, and I am quite sure he will accede to what I wish. Then I shall

VOL. II.   F

place myself in communication with Phillips, as soon as I shall have seen him here; and what he has been unable to accomplish alone may, perhaps, be successful under the united efforts of two persons, who mean so kindly by you, and go to work on your behalf with love and sincere interest; for—you will, I hope, have no objection to my pursuing a twofold object—your reconciliation with your father, and the search for your Ellinor."

At these words, inexpressible emotion and joy almost overpowered Mr. Sidney. He, who was in general so composed, could hardly restrain his feelings. A tear involuntarily coursed down his cheek, and his lips quivered so convulsively that I feared the excess of his joy would betray him."

" Ah ! " said he, in his gentle, kind voice, "ah ! when will the time come when I shall be able to express to you in deeds, and not alone in words, how infinitely I am indebted to you. Yes ! you have restored to my weary heart its best and noblest feeling, belief in an unchanging and merciful Providence, which belief, from the cruel and unnatural conduct of my nearest relations, had been shaken. You have proved to me that this beautiful earth is still inhabited by creatures who deserve to enjoy its blessings; and after having done all this, and in place of an earthly father given me a Heavenly One, and a friend in place of a brother, you will even restore me to my Ellinor ! Ah ! why am I not

THE MADMAN OF ST. JAMES'. 67

yet already master of myself and of my actions?
Why does Heaven still deal so hardly with me, as if
the raging fury of a storm followed me, and me
alone!"

This was the first murmur I had ever heard from
his lips, and only the thought of his Ellinor, torn
from him and, perhaps, insulted, could have called it
forth; but it was also the last; for the noble heart of
this man did not possess the weakness to complain:
he could endure, and when he had endured heroically
all that a man could bear, he could—act.

"Remember," said I, in as convincing, earnest,
and prophetic a manner as I could, "remember the
words of Mr. Graham, the clergyman, when he spoke
of the lake and the blue sky above: 'In those quiet
waters the dark clouds of the stormy sky will one day
be reflected, but they shall pass away, and upon your
head also the cheering beams of the sun of happiness
will one day shed its rays.'"

"Yes," said he, "yes, it will be thus! A dim
foreshadowing assures me that it will be thus: it
never yet deceived me in sorrow, why then should it
deceive me in joy? I feel that the evening of my
misfortunes is come, and the morning of my happiness will soon dawn. But now farewell! Here comes
Mr. Chappert, and shows me his watch; he has
already allowed me to walk longer than the appointed
time; I am still under restraint, but now I can endure
it. One day the hour of freedom will sound, and

F 2

then—and then—Good evening, Mr. Chappert! Yes, yes, I am quite ready. Adieu! Adieu!"

"Adieu!" I rejoined, and we separated. I went to my own room, wrote my letter to Sir John ——, in London, which I sent off the next day, being post day, under the address of one of my most confidential friends, attached to the Prussian embassy in London; and then I began my preparations for being able to set off on my journey at a moment's notice after receiving the expected answer.

Two days after this, sitting at my writing-table, in the morning, I heard a knock at my door. The words "Come in," brought, to my great astonishment and delight, the anxiously-expected Phillips. He carried his pack on his shoulders, thus showing the purpose for which he appeared to have come to me.

I sprang up, and hastened to meet him.

"Good morning, sir!" said he, after first glancing rapidly into my chamber. "Well, here we are together again; but, first of all, how is *he*?"

"All right, all in order!" I said, quickly looking at the honest face of the good man with quite different eyes from what I did formerly, when I did not know his real worth to its full extent.

But this lies in the course of nature; how often do we meet with strangers who arrest our attention by their expressive faces, but in the shifting scenes of life quickly pass away from our recollection, without

THE MADMAN OF ST. JAMES'. 69

having attracted more than this short casual attention. But if we could sometimes guess what jewels lie concealed within the hearts of those strangers, we should hardly have time to read their hearts through their features, and far less to reflect sufficiently on the associations and ideas which their appearance brings to our mind.

Thus, with quite different feelings from formerly, I looked at the man now standing before me. Certainly, after a key had once been given me, it was much easier for me to read the traces of fidelity, devotion, and self-sacrifice in the earnest, energetic, but mild features of that face, which formerly, by superficial observation, seemed only to testify a good-natured, trustworthy, and honest charaċter.

"All in order, you say? Well, sir, you know better now who the Madman of St. James' is?"

"Indeed I do, my good Phillips; and what news do you bring us to-day?"

"Neither good nor bad—that is to say, as good as none."

And then he briefly related to me an account of his exertions and his searches, named to me the places he had fruitlessly visited, the false traces which had misled him, and, finally, those places which he intended again to visit in his wanderings.

"And what do *you* intend to do?" he asked me.

70   THE MADMAN OF ST. JAMES'.

"I shall do what you have been doing so long, and are not yet tired of doing,—seek, and, I hope, find!"

"Find, find, sir; yes, that is the chief point. But when, and where, shall I see you again? Make all your plans now, for I shall not be able to remain here longer than about thirty-six hours; and now I must leave you, for it is known that I am with you."

"Every morning at the same hour you will find me in my room. To-morrow, then, eh?"

He nodded assent.

"And now you are going to him, are you not?"

"To *him;* I understand. Do not mention the other name; we both know him. Ha, ha! Mr. Sidney! Mr. Sidney! But only wait a little; it will be different one day; the time will come when they will all take off their hats before this Mr. Sidney; Mr. Sidney—eh?"

"Yes, yes, it shall be different—it must be, as sure as there is a heaven above us!"

He went to find his master,—his master, who deserved to possess such a servant, and who, perhaps, was anxiously counting the minutes to the time when he should see his honest face again, and hear words from his mouth which reminded him of a happiness which long since had passed away, but now was soon to be restored.

THE MADMAN OF ST. JAMES'. 71

The next morning came, and with it Phillips, his wooden boxes again on his back. We held a rather long and important consultation about what each of us had next to do, and how, and in what manner, we could best arrange it.

On the same day, even before Phillips left, I communicated to Mr. Sidney our plans as soon as I had an opportunity of speaking to him, and I had the pleasure of finding that his opinion coincided with ours in all points; only on some subjects he added a remark, and completed what we had left for him to arrange, assuring us of his perfect approval of all we proposed.

First, with respect to Phillips, he was this time to take a route different from his former fruitless travels; while I was to visit a part which had been less attentively searched by him.

He was to go towards the south, and I, for the present, towards the north of England. But we mutually settled on certain times and places at which we should correspond, and communicate to each other all that occurred.

With respect to the route I should take, Dunsdale Castle was the first place I should visit. There, on Percy's estate, on account of the prolonged absence of the proprietor, great confusion must naturally have prevailed in his affairs, with respect to the stewardship of the agent in London, and the rents paid by the farmers, &c.

72   THE MADMAN OF ST. JAMES'.

What had happened there, or what was supposed
to have become of himself, Percy had never been able
to ascertain. In the beginning of his wanderings,
Phillips had been there twice; but his confidential
position, relative to the Viscount Dunsdale, being
unknown to the steward, he, being unable to furnish
any proofs of it, had only been able to gather the
general opinions of the people living in the neighbourhood; and these were not sufficient to satisfy the
growing anxiety of Percy, particularly as he himself,
in former times, chiefly occupied with himself and
his own misfortunes, had troubled himself very little
about his estates; every quarter a large sum of money,
sufficient for all his wants, being remitted to him
through the director.

But for another reason my visit to Dunsdale Castle
seemed to me to be of the utmost importance; for I
thought that Ellinor, anxious and uncertain as to the
abode of Percy, would, if she were in the position to
write, address herself to Dunsdale Castle. How
valuable the contents of such a letter would be in aid
of my efforts to discover her, Percy immediately
understood, and for that reason gave me a letter to
his old steward, wherein he desired him to permit
me to search for and open all letters and papers without exception, which might have accumulated there
during his long absence; for these letters, if any had
arrived, must have remained unopened, as no one

knew where the viscount was to be found, and each moment news of him, or even his return itself, might be expected. Of the money which I should find in the hands of the steward at Dunsdale Castle, I had been obliged to give the possessor my word of honour to use a portion for the journey which I had undertaken in his behalf; and on my return, I was to bring part of it changed into paper with me; for above all things, ample means must be provided to facilitate his escape from St. James'.

Much as I had objected at first to this proposal, I was obliged later to see the necessity of acceding to Mr. Sidney's urgent request. My own resources were ample for my own travels and residence in England, but for such a large outlay as was required for this suddenly-undertaken journey I was not prepared.

After I had obtained every possible information at Dunsdale Castle, and in Percy's name finished my business there, and had, lastly, communicated to the old steward of this almost princely domain as much about the residence and return of his master as appeared to be suitable to our purpose, I should proceed on my journey towards the seat of the Marquis of Seymour, at Codrington, and if I found him there, which, according to the account given by Phillips, seemed pretty certain, I should immediately begin my operations on Percy's father him-

THE MADMAN OF ST. JAMES'.

self,—but with him only, not with Lord Mortimer,
—in order to forward that object which I had
sworn to Percy to endeavour to bring about as soon
as possible.

If *successful* in this attempt, which we both
hoped, I was then to return to St. James' as quickly
as I could, furnished with authority from the marquis
to put an end to his son's detention; return then
with Percy to his father, and afterwards begin our
search for Ellinor.

But if *un*successful, I should then, without loss
of time, proceed to London and address myself at once
to the legal adviser of the viscount; and, assisted by
Sir William Graham, the barrister, take all the necessary steps for legal proceedings, of which I should
inform Mr. Sidney, in St. James', through Phillips;—
only in the greatest case of necessity I was to write
to Sidney himself; and then the letter, without
addressing him by any name or using any signature,
should be sent for him directed to the wife of
Chappert.

When once the action had commenced, and I saw
that all the persons engaged in it were favourably
disposed towards their client, I should then also return to St. James', in order, with the assistance of
Phillips and Chappert, whom Sidney hoped to
gain over entirely by that time, to arrange his
escape.

THE MADMAN OF ST. JAMES. 75

But if I in my various journeys found Ellinor and her father, I was then to take them to London to Sir William Graham, or to Dunsdale Castle, whichever they preferred. Should I, however, receive any intelligence of their place of residence, then, putting for the time every thing else aside, I should follow up their traces until I had found them and placed them in safety.

This was a sketch of my journey and its objects: one may perceive that I had undertaken business enough, and that it required all possible patience and attention to bring about a favourable result.

But that I should not undertake this long and troublesome journey alone, and should not feel the want of necessary assistance from a willing companion, Mr. Sidney, as well as Phillips, had proposed that I should take the eldest son of the latter with me as my servant. He was at present at school, under the care of a clergyman in the country, whose house was situated on my road to Dunsdale; and when I passed that way, if I should find him likely to suit me, and willing to go, I was to take him with me immediately. For Phillips had come this time without his sons, partly because the two boys were troublesome to him on his long marches, and partly because he saw that the education of his children could not be attended to with such a wandering mode of life. In their place, therefore, he had bought a couple of large dogs to draw his cart, such as are used in different parts of England by persons of his calling. They were strong animals, and quick enough to perform all that was required of them with ease, without causing so much inconvenience as a horse.

CHAPTER IV.

DEPARTURE FROM ST. JAMES'.

Thus far, as the reader will see, everything had been carefully considered and prepared, and it only required the arrival of the anxiously-expected letter to set me off, as I was quite ready for my journey. And for this I had not to wait long; for that good Sir John ——, in London, notwithstanding his many occupations and indifferent health, had been punctual and good-natured enough to accede at once to my very extraordinary request.

Phillips was already on his way towards the south, and between Mr. Sidney and myself everything necessary had been arranged. About a week after Phillips had left, a little party, consisting of the director, the doctors, several of the official members, and some of the most reasonable of the patients, amongst whom were Mr. Sidney, the Baronet, and the Prince of Denmark, had assembled together in the great skittle-ground of the park, on a warm and rather misty afternoon, to give themselves up to the enjoyment of this favourite game.

It was post day, and I had already several times climbed up the little hill close by to look out for the well-known yellow cart, and at last I saw it coming along the broad road at its usual speed.

I slowly returned to our party, giving a sign to Mr. Sidney that the post had come in, and that therefore we had perhaps again advanced a step nearer towards the fulfilment of our wishes.

In less than half an hour appeared the post-boy, bringing in his large bag a whole heap of letters, which, being mostly for those who were here present, were delivered to them at once.

For me there were three letters ;—two from friends in London and Germany, and the third was the one so anxiously expected from Sir John ——, in London.

Each person who had received a letter seated himself somewhat apart from the others to read it. After quietly reading mine, I got up, approached the director, and handing him Sir John's letter, said, in such a natural and calm voice that afterwards I was quite surprised at it myself,—

" See, Mr. Elliotson, I have got to give you a friendly greeting from Sir John ——; but unfortunately this greeting is accompanied by something else which really grieves me."

Mr. Elliotson took the letter, and read it silently to the end. It contained the following lines, word for word :—

" My very worthy young friend,—Supposing that

these lines will find you still at St. James', I send
you my kindest remembrances, with the request that,
as soon as the pleasures you there enjoy will allow
you, you will wend your way back to me. Some important news for you, which I have just received from
Hamburg, but which I do not like to communicate
to you in writing, is the cause of this request.

"Relying on the anxiety you will naturally feel to
receive further information on the subject, I regret
at the same time to be thus obliged to call you away
from a place where I know from experience such a
comfortable life is led, and which seems to please you
well, to judge from your long stay; at the same time,
for my own sake, I am glad that this matter has occurred, since it gives me the pleasure of seeing you
again so soon. Give my friendly compliments to Mr.
Elliotson, Mr. Lorenz, and Mr. Derby—merry little
Mr. Derby,—and begging you to accept the assurance
of my regard and friendship, I remain always,

"Your sincere old friend,

"JOHN ———."

"I am indeed sorry, for our sakes," said the director, when he had finished the letter. "Ha! the old
boy has written it himself, so it must be of some consequence; but what a trembling hand he writes now
—that good old Sir John!"

"Have you known him long?" I asked, just for
the sake of saying something.

"Oh, yes! formerly he often came here, and it was here, in fact, that the foundation of his learning, experience, and success in life was laid; he is a good old gentleman; but I am really very sorry that you are obliged to go away so soon."

Those present now came round me, and hearing what was the matter, they all expressed to me in various ways their regret at seeing me leave St. James' so quickly and unexpectedly.

"And when do you think of leaving?" asked Mr. Lorenz, who had suddenly appeared to become very thoughtful at the mention of Sir John's name, and who, as if at variance with himself about some half-formed resolution, had been walking several times up and down apart from the others. "When do you think of going, sir? I have—I should like to ask Sir John a question, and would ask you to deliver a letter to him."

"To-morrow, to-morrow, my dear Mr. Lorenz," I replied, "if I can only possibly get ready by that time."

"Ah!" cried Mr. Derby, who in the mean time had been exchanging a few words in a low voice with the Colonel, "then you will not see the performance of our tragedy?"

"I shall return as soon as I possibly can," was my answer; "at least I hope not to be long away; and shall perhaps be back in time to be able to admire your performances."

THE MADMAN OF ST. JAMES'. 81

With these words I turned towards the Colonel and his companions, and bowed to them all in a friendly manner; they acknowledged it, smiled after their fashion, and shook hands with me.

"And, under these circumstances," I continued, turning to the director, "would you allow me to leave the greater part of my luggage here?"

"By all means," replied Mr. Elliotson; "to be sure! Your room remains still yours during your absence; come back when you like, and the sooner the better; you will be as welcome as when you first came; and if you will allow me," added he very politely, "may I offer you the use of my carriage as far as the first station?"

"Pray do not trouble yourself, sir," I answered; "you know I am a good walker, and in the same way as I came I can return; travelling alone has always had a peculiar charm for me."

"Allow me to make you a proposal," said the Madman of St. James', who had until now been silent. "If you will do me a favour, take my horse; it will be a pleasure for me in this way to hasten your journey, and make it more agreeable to you."

I looked up at the speaker and the bystanders somewhat surprised, for I was indeed astonished at this proposal, although it was by no means a disagreeable one.

"If I did not fear to deprive you of an amusement, Mr. Sidney," I answered, bowing, "I would

VOL. II.   G with pleasure take advantage of your kind offer; but ——"

"Take it, take it!" said Mr. Derby; "it is always more agreeable to ride than to walk; Mr. Sidney would not have offered it to you if it had not given him pleasure to do so."

"Well, then, I accept your offer with pleasure!" said I, addressing Mr. Sidney, and pressing his hand.

"That is right!" said the director; "and now, as this affair is so far arranged, gentlemen, let us return to our game; the days are long, and you will still have time enough this evening for your packing."

Nobody made any objection, so we resumed our game. But I must confess, for my part, my thoughts were already far away, as also were the thoughts of him, whose renewed hopes, sailing once more over the broad sea of life, went with me on the way which led to their realization.

Thus had arrived the moment when, after a residence of nearly six weeks in St. James', contrary to all my former plans, I was, in this unexpected and extraordinary manner, about to undertake a new journey, the duration of which I could not guess, and the distance of which at present was not to be calculated.

It was on the twentieth of July, at eight o'clock in the morning, after having the evening before paid a

THE MADMAN OF ST. JAMES'. 83

visit to all those to whom I owed this attention, that I entered the park, where I found those already assembled who had the intention of accompanying me a little on my way. One of the servants was at the door with the horse, which was saddled, and furnished with a little valise.

It was indeed a noble and beautiful animal, of the most brilliant and glossy black; not a single white hair was to be seen on his slender and graceful body. He was rather small, as the thorough-bred Arab always is, but in every respect most beautifully shaped; he was, moreover, extremely intelligent and docile, and appeared to be much less fitted for a toilsome journey, than to shine in some circus as a model of beauty and swiftness. It was, however, Percy's wish that I should make use of this his favourite horse, and I acceded to it.

Besides Percy, there were waiting for me at the door the director, the chaplain, and several others; the doctors were gone on their daily rounds, and had already taken leave of me early in the morning.

"Walk on with the horse, Simonds," said the director to the servant, who was holding Bravour by the bridle; "we will accompany the gentleman a little way on foot; and you, Mr. Sidney, will you not go with us too, just to see how the doctor looks on your horse?"

" With pleasure, if I may be allowed the honour," answered Mr. Sidney, and he walked by my side

G 2

84   THE MADMAN OF ST. JAMES'.

behind the others, who were going on slowly a little
in advance, discussing the beauty and the qualifications of Bravour, my new travelling companion.

"But really," said I in a loud voice, so that all
might hear it, "I am rather anxious about the result
of my introduction to your Bravour. I hope I shall
not find him too unmanageable; for although I am
not a bad rider, still he has been accustomed to such
a perfect one."

"Do not be in the least afraid," answered Mr.
Sidney; "he is fiery, spirited, and quick, but he has
no vice; and what he is capable of doing, you will
soon find out. Were it not for appearance you
would not require spurs. A word is sufficient to set
him off, and to give him wings, if necessary."

We then walked on a little while beside each other
without speaking. I was silent, for indeed the
separation from the beloved friend in whose soul I
had so deeply read, and whom I had learned to love
so truly, lay heavy on my heart; while he walked
by my side, apparently unconcerned, and even almost
more cheerful than usual.

"You appear very serious to-day, Robert," resumed he, in a low voice, touching my arm, as he
usually did when speaking to me in confidence;
"does any thought or anxiety weigh on your mind?"

"Yes, Percy, the thought that I must part from *you*."

"Nothing else? and that is just what rejoices me.
You go to return again, and how will you return!

THE MADMAN OF ST. JAMES'. 85

Yes, I must confess to you, it is long since I have had such a happy hour as this parting hour is; for it is the commencement of action, of new activity, of——"

He was going to speak further, but some thought seemed to stop him.

" Ah!" continued he, somewhat subdued, "how happy are you! Could I but go with you—go with you into the glorious free world—but, but, it cannot be; let us await the future, and what it may bring us."

" Have you still anything to say to me?" I asked, for I remarked how our companions on before were walking more slowly. "If you have, say it quickly; we shall soon be interrupted."

" No," he answered firmly; "I have nothing more to say, for you know all; and I am convinced that you will do all that is right. I have the greatest confidence in your present undertaking, for it seems to be as if no one could have a better chance of success than yourself."

" May it be just as you say, and may the will of Providence be in accordance with our wishes; nobody would rejoice more sincerely than I."

We were here interrupted. Mr. Elliotson called out loudly,—

" Listen, Mr. Sidney, listen! We have just been disputing how many miles your friend could trot in a day with your horse—what is your opinion?"

We approached, and Mr. Sidney smiled; he knew his horse.

"That depends upon the rider," said he, "and whether the road is good, and if he is properly cared for. How many miles do *you* think he could go?"

"Well, I should think he might do from twenty to twenty-five miles on such a road as the one to London."

"And I would take it upon myself, without using either whip or spur, to go for three weeks from thirty to forty miles with him; but that depends, as I have already said, very much upon the rider."

They expressed astonishment, and would not quite believe, disputed, and came at last to the usual result of a wager. We now arrived at the end of the grounds of St. James', and it was time to part. Here we stopped, spoke a few words of friendly farewell, and shook hands. Mr. Sidney was the last who took leave of me. I did not dare say more to him, but we needed no words to understand each other; a pressure of the hand, a look was enough.

Bravour was led forward. When I had mounted, the intelligent animal turned his beautiful head and his brilliant eyes round to his master, as if to say, "And will you not go away with me yourself this time?"

One more farewell, one more greeting, and I was slowly riding up the broad road towards the hill.

My heart felt oppressed; I rode on without think-

THE MADMAN OF ST. JAMES'. 87

ing of anything particular until I arrived at the point where the road overlooks the top of the hill, and I could see from thence St. James' for the last time.

There stood that large beautiful building, a bright spot in the rich green foliage of the old trees which surrounded it. What were my feelings now? What had I not heard and experienced in the short space of a few weeks?

I looked searchingly towards the park, as far as my eye could see; I looked for something—at first in vain; at last I saw it wave upon the well-known hill—a white handkerchief. I waved mine, and signalled a hundred friendly farewells in return, for I knew from whom it came, and to whom it was sent. One more look, still one more greeting, and turning my horse's head, I rode in the direction of the north of old England, leaving the road to London on my right. And now, for the first time, I felt I was once more at liberty, that I was free, and with a deep sigh I said to myself, "Why are not all masters of themselves, as I am, and able to use the powers which God has given to them; and what have I done to be thus happy?"

CHAPTER V.

A TOLERABLY GOOD BEGINNING TO A DIFFICULT JOURNEY.

A JOURNEY on horseback through the most beautiful parts of England does not offer to a reflective mind many opportunities for *ennui*, even if the traveller have no higher purpose than to amuse himself by the change of scene. The smiling freshness of the woods and fields, the ground ornamented with trees of a century's growth, the young shrubs, the softly undulating hills, the teeming fruitful valleys, as well as the shady forest, sometimes intersected with dark monotonous moors, present such a variegated, charming, and luxuriant picture for reflection, that at each turn of the road one may imagine he is entering another country. But no such agreeable impressions did these scenes make upon me; from the first moment I was alone, the purpose of my present journey had so entirely filled my mind, that at the beginning I was completely incapable of paying the least attention to what surrounded me, much less to connect it with the thoughts which seemed to course each other through my mind. Although I had not for one moment deceived myself as to the difficulties attending my voluntarily-undertaken task, having considered every point of it before starting, still a long solitary journey was well calculated to draw all my thoughts and all the powers of my mental faculties into this one direction. And when I accurately ran over all the particulars, and thereby brought my mind into a more clear and favourable state for action, I still felt no great relief. I saw myself deeply involved in a labyrinth of inhuman passions, pushed into the very midst of them, and thrown completely on my own resources. I hardly felt myself strong and clever enough to arrive at the wished-for end happily and to the satisfaction of all who were connected with it.

Fortunately, however, this state of feeling, after a few days of reflection and exercise, was dispelled triumphantly by my own happy disposition, and the natural cheerfulness of my mind. From my earliest youth, from education as well as from inclination, I had ever been passionately interested in the secret working and creations of nature. In former days a romantic, in later days a faithful observer, through diligent study I had become acquainted with her glorious voice; and once initiated into her wonders, I had long accustomed myself to the influence and magic of her charms.

All that surrounded me—the trees, the hills, the valleys, the rain, the sunshine, the breezes, the solemn silence—all seemed even to speak to me; and I understood this lovely, wonderful language.

It was therefore no wonder it was a pleasure for me, without wishing for or thinking of anything else, to plunge into the rich depths of these treasures, and endeavour to penetrate to the source of that, which is ever the object of the struggles of the human heart, which, however, like the stone of Sisyphus, is never to reach the top of the mountain.

And as in my youth I had been taught to observe and understand nature, in later years I wished as a man, particularly in my profession as a physician, to study and understand mankind, which is nothing more than nature in miniature; having like her its sunshine, its storms, its light and shadows, its spring and winter. When I entered into any new connection with a stranger, I immediately endeavoured to understand his capacities, his inclinations, and ambitions. I tried to place myself in his situation and circumstances, and endeavoured to act after his ideas; and, by continued and unwearied practice in this, I had often been successful in finding out exactly the character of the man, and knew perfectly well how I was to treat him.

This knowledge, I confess, sometimes deceived me; for many show themselves under such a thick impervious veil, that all efforts of this kind are in

THE MADMAN OF ST. JAMES'. 91

vain; but on the whole I had the pleasure of reaping some advantage from this mental speculation; it benefited me, and I often gained the confidence of those with whom I occupied myself.

It has ever been one of my favourite employments (and I believe I have already mentioned this before) to judge of a man by his exterior, and from that to draw, if not an opinion, at least a conjecture, as to his intellectual and moral qualities and disposition.

There can be nothing more interesting for a physician than to observe carefully the wonderful play of the features in healthy and sick persons, and to compare this faithfully with their mental qualifications. Very many physicians have occupied themselves with this scientific study before me, and out of it have arisen the so-called physiognomical-diagnostic degrees of illness, in which they went so far as to state that every illness, as well as each passion, produces a certain expression of the face, a certain peculiar look. I will not affirm this, nor even defend it; for pain does not always express itself differently on the face according to the place or cause of suffering, but only in proportion to the individual sensitiveness of the sufferer, and his bodily and moral strength. For me only the individual expression and features of the patients were interesting, and as I carried on this favourite employment both with the suffering and with the healthy, I moved continually in a large circle, searching, thinking, and imagining nature and mankind. I was at home with both ; both gave me of theirs, and to both I gave of mine.

But I must not lose myself in this labyrinth of anthropological medical speculation; very many readers, not only those who are easily tired, want to hear nothing of medical reflections; and so I return to my quiet journey, my silent observations, and particularly to the tranquillity of mind I felt when the beauty, the freshness, and the power of nature began to exercise their influence on my oppressed heart, and withdrew me from the morbid feelings which an excited imagination had occasioned.

I was thus quite restored to the charms of the present, and, above all else, I bestowed the greatest care on the horse confided to me by the hand of friendship, —the horse which stepped as lightly and spiritedly beneath me, as if he had only a journey of a few hours instead of many weeks, before him. I always attended to him myself, and spoke to him, and caressed him, as I had seen Mr. Sidney do ; never letting him feel a strong hand, but allowing him to go on his own way. We soon perfectly understood each other, and I became much attached to the noble animal, who was soon as contented and cheerful as I felt myself to be.

The first two days' journey I had taken leisurely, for I must first accustom myself to this kind of travelling; I went, therefore, only about twenty miles a-day, which Bravour seemed scarcely to feel.

On the third day, however, I went about twenty-five, and on the fourth I was obliged to hurry still more, in order to reach my night's lodging at the house of the village clergyman to whom the charge of the pedlar's sons had been entrusted.

At about twelve o'clock on this day, I came to a very pretty part of the country, which, watered by a river, has always been one of the most populous and industrious places in England. Around me I saw large factories, the chimneys black with smoke, day and night performing their work of machinery, never tired, never sleepy, but always groaning, as if they felt the trouble of being kept in constant motion. What has not the inventive mind and all-subduing hand of man produced!

Between them, placed at intervals, were cheerful-looking farmhouses, and sometimes could be seen the beautiful estate of some rich nobleman; but everywhere the people were in full work, occupied in earning the bread which, when gained by one's own labour, tastes so sweet.

After I had partaken of some refreshment in a village where I stopped, I saddled my horse, and, after having inquired for the best road, I again mounted, and trotted off in the direction which had been pointed out to me. Gradually the vicinity assumed a more rural appearance; all the fields through which I rode waved with corn nearly ripe. In many places I found the labourers already making their preparations for harvest; and at last, at five o'clock in the afternoon, I discovered from afar the village where the clergyman whom I sought resided.

The white church-tower peeped forth from the trees which surrounded it, and a number of tame pigeons were flying about over the low brown roofs of the houses, which were planted round with lime-trees, and the gardens enclosed with regular, well-cut hedges.

I approached slowly, making my way through the crowd of village children, who had quickly assembled full of curiosity. I soon found myself in the middle of the village, where, opposite the churchyard, I came upon the quiet, unpretending little house of the clergyman, which, built of brick like the other houses, was distinguished only by a green painted railing before the door.

Just as I had dismounted, and fastened the bridle of my horse to a wooden post, a rosy-cheeked, curly-headed, sturdy boy of about sixteen years of age noisily rushed out of the door, whom I immediately recognized as my old acquaintance Bob, the eldest son of our good Phillips.

Not my arrival, but the arrival of a beautiful horse, had called him forth; but as soon as he had more particularly looked at me, he also recognized me, and said,—

"Ah, sir! is it you? Well, I did not expect that;

and what a beautiful horse! Ah, it is much better to ride than to walk."

"That was just my opinion," said I smiling; "and, therefore, I have come on horseback. But how are you, Bob; and how is little Will, your brother?"

"Oh, quite well, thank you, sir. Have you seen my father lately?"

"Yes, Bob; and it is upon his account I have come here. And I hope you will be glad to hear some good news of him."

"Well, sir, does he want me to draw the waggon again?" asked the boy, looking at me inquiringly.

"Nothing of the kind. But first of all, where is Mr. Smith, the clergyman?"

"Come in, sir; he is not come home yet; but he will be in directly, for he went into the fields about two hours ago to look at the corn."

He opened the door for me, and we entered a neat little room, strewn with white sand, and with oak furniture. At a window sat an elderly woman, industriously occupied in turning her spinning wheel; but as soon as we entered she got up, and came to meet us.

"Good evening, my good woman," I said, offering my hand. "I hear Mr. Smith, the clergyman, is not at home; I hope, however, that you will allow me to wait for him here."

"With pleasure, sir," replied the housekeeper, for

such she was; and she placed a chair, covered with brown leather, for me at the table.

"Will you let me take the horse to the stable, sir?" asked Bob, who, anticipating an answer in the affirmative, held the latch of the door in his hand. "The boys there outside, full of curiosity, are all standing round that good Bravour, who, although very good-natured, is still only a horse."

"What," I asked, "do you know the horse?"

"Why, sir, a horse like this, which I have often fed myself, and stroked when I was quite a little fellow, as if I should not know him again! My Lord Percy often let me ride upon him when I was only about as big as that." And with his hand he showed me how tall he thought that was.

"Go and take him to the stable, then," said I to the boy, who, the longer I looked at him, appeared to become still more intelligent, bold, and strong; and he spoke to me, and frankly looked at me with his large blue eyes, just as his father would have done, had he been in his place.

The boy sprang to the door, threw a cloth over the horse's back, and amid the joyful voices of the children standing around, led him through the great gate into the stable. Ten minutes afterwards he was again in the house.

"Well, Bob, have you seen to him properly?"

"Yes, sir! yes; and I really believe Bravour

THE MADMAN OF ST. JAMES'. 97

knew me, for he neighed directly I began to stroke his neck as I used to do."

"Then I think Bravour is nearly as intelligent as you are. But, now tell me, how do you occupy yourself here?"

"I read, write, listen to Mr. Smith's sermons, and then I learn history, and geography, and arithmetic. But as for arithmetic, sir, I do not like that much."

"Tout comme chez nous!" thought I, and laughed heartily at the candour of the boy.

"Altogether, then, you like to be in a field better than at a writing table?" I asked, looking at him significantly.

The boy smiled, and glanced at the old woman, who now began,—

"Yes, sir! Will learns much better; Bob is only quicker in action and louder in speech than he."

"Can you ride?" I asked.

The boy now became crimson, hesitated in his reply, and winked with one eye towards the spot where the housekeeper was seated.

She now immediately assumed a very serious demeanour, and said in a less jesting but still good-humoured voice,—

"With respect to that, sir, you have asked a question which, this evening, when Mr. Smith returns, will be seriously discussed."

"Why so?"

"Why, I love Bob very much, for he is a good

VOL II.   H

boy, even if he is at times a little too wild; but he has prepared a vexation for Mr. Smith during his absence, which will draw upon him a sharp rebuke, and, perhaps, even a punishment."

"Why, heavens!" cried Bob, in a very delighted, half-comic, half-tragic tone, "and all this is about having ridden a colt."

"Yes, but to ride it until it was half dead and stiff, I should think, was more than enough!" answered the old woman angrily.

"Half dead?" said the boy, and he laughed outright; "just listen to that; a half-dead horse would not enjoy his oats as well as he does now in the stable; could he, sir, if he were half dead?"

"Be quiet, Bob; I say what I said before, that ——"

"And have you really been doing so, Bob?" I asked seriously.

"No, sir! no. To tell you the truth, I was wandering about in the meadow behind, when the colt, which is really, however, not much of a colt, came on the clover which belongs to us, and not to the neighbour who owns the horse. By all means, I thought to myself, it is better to take a little ride upon the neighbour's colt, rather than he should eat up the clover which belongs to his reverence, and so I put a bridle on him, and let him trot about a little, and that is the whole story, sir, if you want to know it."

THE MADMAN OF ST. JAMES'. 99

"Trot!" repeated the old lady, now really angry, "why, he made it jump, sir, jump over the shafts of the large waggon until it could jump no longer—yes, indeed—don't laugh at it, boy; and then—but here comes the minister himself."

The front door creaked, and immediately the Rev. Mr. Smith entered—a grey-headed little man of venerable appearance, dressed in a black frock-coat, with large buttons; his hat and stick in one hand, and a bunch of wild flowers in the other. His face was mild and pleasing, and his whole appearance bore the stamp of a true English pastor of the good old times. Before I could speak to him, Will followed him in, shook me by the hand, and cried out in a joyful tone,—

"See, your reverence, this is the gentleman about whom I was telling you the other day, who gave us the shilling, and helped us to push the cart."

"Good evening, sir!" said I, offering my hand to the clergyman, who bade me welcome.

"And what procures for me the pleasure of such an agreeable visit?" he asked, in a voice as gentle as was his appearance.

"If you will allow me, sir, I have to give you a letter, and I bring a request from the father of these two boys. Could I speak a few words to you alone?"

"Certainly, certainly—come in here!"

And he opened the door of another room, in which

he generally wrote his sermons. It was, if possible, still more simply furnished than the other, and looked just as the study of such a good, simple-hearted, country clergyman ought to look. There was a large writing table of walnut-wood, and an armchair before it; round the room were shelves filled with books, and above the writing table hung a beautiful engraving of the Holy Sacrament, and on the chimney-piece stood a black cross of cast-iron; this comprised all the furniture and ornament of this little room.

I had just time to take notice of all this while Mr. Smith was reading the letter I had given him. As soon as he had finished, he folded it up, and said,—

"So you have then come, sir, to take my good Bob away from me? Well, I can say nothing against it; but I should have liked to have kept him a little longer. But it is all right as it is; and may God bless you and him, and give His blessing to what you undertake."

"Thank you, sir, with all my heart. Has Bob been confirmed?"

"Oh, yes; six months ago—before he came to me. The boy has got plenty of intelligence, but he has not so much patience and perseverance as his brother Will; but he will be very useful to you. Would you not like to speak with him at once, and hear what he says to the arrangement?"

On my answer in the affirmative, Mr. Smith opened the door, and called Bob, who immediately appeared, but with rather a sorrowful face; for, most likely, he was thinking about the over-ridden colt, and the lectures were always received in this solemn-looking room.

"Listen, my good Bob," began the clergyman, kindly: "this gentleman here, whom you already know, has brought me news from your father, and wishes to have you as his servant, or, if you like it better, as his companion on the journey he is about to undertake. I knew before the gentleman came that you had long since been selected for this appointment —at least, that you were to enter the service of the Viscount of Dunsdale; but as this gentleman is now engaged in some affairs of his lordship's, and it makes very little difference if you go a few months earlier or later, I therefore ask you if you would like to go with him, and will you always be faithful and ready and willing to do all that may be required of you?"

"Yes, sir, yes," answered Bob, quickly. "I should like to go very much. What, and am I to go directly? That is just what I should like!"

"And on horseback, too," I added; "for we must both of us be mounted."

"Hurrah!" cried the boy, jumping for joy. "To ride with you through England? That is just what I have longed for, and Will has often laughed at me about it. That will be glorious! glorious! Yes,

yes, sir, I will, indeed, be faithful and obedient, and never forget all your good advice; but I will think of you, and pray for you, just as I always pray for father and the Viscount of Dunsdale."

"That is right, my son," replied the good old man; and, as if to bless him, he laid his hand on the boy's head.

We then returned to the sitting-room, where the old housekeeper had prepared supper, consisting of milk, eggs, cheese, ham, and fish, and then she heard that I was to be her master's guest for the night.

"Here, Will," cried Bob to his brother, placing a whole pile of books before him on the table, "these are all for you; and I don't want anything for them, for I shall not want them any more."

"What, Bob! are you really going away, then?"

"Yes; and with the doctor there and Bravour, and a horse of my own, and, hurrah! we are going all through England."

We listened, and laughed at the merry humour of the boy, who really promised to be fit for something.

"It could not be otherwise," remarked Mr. Smith; "he is the true son of his father."

During supper, we spoke of what it was necessary to procure for Bob; and, in the first place, the neighbouring farmer was sent for to arrange about the purchase of a suitable horse, and the village tailor received an order to prepare immediately the proper clothes.

The farmer now came, and hearing that we wanted a horse, thought proper to forget the trick Bob had lately played him, and recommended his strong, somewhat large, sorrel-coloured pony, and we paid for him—saddle and bridle included—the sum of eighteen pounds four shillings, while Bob, like an experienced judge of horse-flesh, first examined the horse's mouth, and then expressed his satisfaction. When the tailor came, I asked Bob what articles of clothing he wanted.

"Nothing more, sir," said he, "than a pair of top-boots and spurs, a pair of buckskin breeches with bright buttons, and just such a light grey coat as yours; I have got everything else."

"Bless the boy!" I cried; "the breeches and the coat you can have if you like, but where on earth are we to get top-boots and spurs in this village?"

"If there is money for it," was the answer, "the boots can be got too. Three doors off lives Mr. Touton, the shoemaker, and he has got just such a pair of boots in his window."

We could not help laughing again at the boy; he knew so well how to help himself. The clothes were ordered, and the tailor promised to let us have them on the evening of the following day. On this account I was obliged to remain a second night at Mr. Smith's, which, for my horse's sake, I did not at all regret.

104   THE MADMAN OF ST. JAMES'.

At last, however, the hour of departure arrived; Bob was booted and spurred, had on his buckskins and the grey coat, and not even the first groom of her Majesty could have mounted his horse with better grace than he did.

The good clergyman and Will, whose eyes were full of tears, accompanied us to the gate, and, followed by their good wishes and prayers, we rode away, on a beautiful July morning, through the fragrant green of the cornfields and meadows, which Bob loved so well.

CHAPTER VI.

A LETTER LOST WHICH CONTAINS IMPORTANT NEWS.

As long as we passed by the houses in the village, and Bob saw here and there a well-known face, he nodded and greeted with hand and mouth; but when we left the last house with its green hedge behind us, he turned all his attention with renewed delight to his spirited little horse, his riding equipments, and the new whip, and then again to his long-wished-for articles of clothing, the buckskins, the spurs, and yellow gloves; but when he had fully examined and admired them all, he became serious, and turning to me, who had been riding in silence beside him, amused with observing him, he looked at me inquiringly, and then at last, unable to restrain himself from asking the question which had been long on his lips, he said smiling,—

"And now, sir, where are we going?"

"Ah, indeed, Bob, I was just going to tell you, but you were still so much occupied with other matters. Do you know Lord Percy, Viscount of Dunsdale?"

"To be sure I do, sir. Why, when I was staying with my aunt he lived in the same house with us."

"And his lady, do you know her too, eh?"

"Oh, Miss Ellinor! Yes, sir; why, I knew her long before I knew Lord Percy. She was the daughter of Mr. Graham, the clergyman of Codrington."

"The same. She was very beautiful, Bob, was she not? Do you not remember that?"

"Why should I not, sir? and such a nice lady, too! I often saw her when she gathered flowers in the wood, or rode out with her father; but the last time I saw her she was going with my Lord Percy to be married, and then, although her beautiful eyes were red as if she had been crying a good deal, she still looked like a real living angel. I was allowed even to kiss her hand when she got into the carriage. My aunt often told me I was a happy fellow to be able to look forward later to enter her service, for I was brought up for that; and although she was only the daughter of a clergyman, who will, however, one day, they say, be a baronet, yet all good people must love and respect her, as they would respect and love the grandest and most beautiful lady. My aunt used to say that to us, sir, and she cried when she said it."

"Well," thought I, "this Miss Ellinor must indeed have been very beautiful to have made such an impression on a boy;" and while thinking of

THE MADMAN OF ST. JAMES'. 107

this, I lost myself again for a moment in the events which Percy had related to me, and which the boy, by his simple, natural description, had awakened in my mind afresh.

"And what do you know of her later fate?" I asked after a pause.

"Nothing more, sir, but that she had a great misfortune, and directly after the marriage was separated from her husband, the Lord Viscount; but where she is I don't know, nor why it happened either."

"But you would recognize her again, would you not, if you were to meet her anywhere, or by chance see her face?"

"That I should, sir, as sure as my name is Bob. She was the only beautiful lady I have ever seen in all my life."

"And do you remember her father also?"

"Yes, sir, even better than I do her, or at least quite as well. He often used to visit Lord Percy on his little pony, which was called Dick, and I always had to ride him gently about until he got cool, for Mr. Graham was always in a hurry; and sometimes he used to give me something, for which I am still very much obliged to him."

"Well, then, listen, my good Bob; know first of all that one chief reason of my journey is to find out these two persons, who are very dear to me."

"What do you say, sir? Well, I will help you, then. I will look out if I see them coming."

"Ah, only have patience, my boy. They are not likely to be on the road to meet us."

"Perhaps not; but I will still look out."

"That is right; but now I will tell you where we are going to first, if you will promise me something which I am now going to ask you."

The boy looked at me attentively. I continued,—

"I have important reasons, Bob, for keeping my journey and its purpose in some degree a secret. You must not speak to anybody about it without my permission."

"Here is my hand on it, sir!" cried the boy heartily; and he offered me his gloved hand. "And now where are we going to first?"

"To Dunsdale Castle."

"Ah, Dunsdale Castle, in the county of ——"

"Do you know this place also?"

"No, sir; I have only heard my father mention it when he was talking about it to Mr. Smith."

"One more question, my good Bob," said I. "Do you know the Marquis of Seymour too — the father?"

"Oh, that I do, sir! He was our *black man* when we lived at my aunt's."

"Black man! What do you mean?"

"Why, we had a game called 'the black man;' and when we played at it, instead of saying 'the black man comes,' we used to say 'Lord Seymour comes.' Ha! if he had only known that!—because he was always swearing, and used to make his gamekeepers threaten us with the whip, if we happened sometimes to start a rabbit from his cover, and hunt it into ours."

" Indeed ! He was very cross, then?"

" Just like his son, sir, Lord Mortimer; he was a dreadful tyrant. Why, it was he who shot poor Othello in the paw."

" Why, Bob, how do you know about that ?"

" A forester, who was there at the time, told aunt of it afterwards; but he only told it after father was gone and Lord Percy too."

" And should you know Othello again ?"

" Of course, sir. Why, I ought to know my old companion, that beautiful large black Othello, with his tremendous teeth and long tail."

" I am glad of it," I said. " And now I will tell you that I also think of paying a visit to your black man, the Marquis of Seymour."

" What ! going to see him at Codrington Hall?"

" Just so, if I find he is there," I replied.

" Good heavens ! why, then, I can call and see my old aunt Ursula !"

" You shall have my permission to do so when we get there; besides, I shall most likely remain some days at Codrington Hall."

" Indeed, sir! that is beyond all my hopes. Why, I like this journey now better than ever."

Such was the style of our first conversation, which

I communicate to the reader, as perhaps it may be of some interest to him.

The first two days we travelled at our leisure, for I would not let Bob suffer any inconvenience from his long-wished-for journey, and I wished also to spare the horses. Besides, in these two days I had full opportunity to feel satisfied at having chosen Bob as my travelling companion; for the boy showed himself so willing and clever, particularly in the care he took of the horses, and was so attentive and obliging in all matters which could add to my convenience, that I liked him better every hour.

Even his simple and lively chatter amused and pleased me; it proved that he already began to form his own opinions, which, under any circumstances, were not to be despised; for generally they were the most natural ones. He also understood perfectly well the peculiar language of the country people who met us, with which I was not conversant, and he always knew how to obtain from each person just what information he wanted.

At the end of our fourth day's journey we heard that Dunsdale was just before us, and that our first point, Dunsdale Castle itself, was only about fifteen miles distant from the place where we halted.

We began our journey the next morning very early, as much to avoid the scorching heat of the day as to arrive at our destination before dinner. It was a beautiful morning; we had trotted for about half

THE MADMAN OF ST. JAMES'. 111

an hour away from our night's lodging, when, at some distance from each other, behind a trench, we saw six large mounds of earth, which immediately indicated to us where we were.

We struck off on a beautiful path; the grass was like a carpet under the feet of our horses; art could not have made it more soft and beautiful, and it covered the black fruitful earth for miles together. The fragrant shades of the thickly-grown oak forest, such as I have never seen equalled in my life, cooled us most delightfully after our hot ride in the burning rays of the sun.

The trees under which we rode were centuries old; their branches, like black serpents, bent from their trunks into the very middle of the broad path, thus forming a roof of foliage, gilded by the rays of the sun, but scarcely allowing the light to pierce through it.

I stopped my horse. I felt my heart beat louder; I was now on the estate of the man to whom, for the moment, I had devoted all my energies, and whose memory filled my whole heart.

Ah! those lovely shades had never cooled his burning brow; the quiet, caressing rustling of the leaves of these old trees, and the cheerful songs of the numerous birds which nestled among them, had never reached his ears! Pining in a more melancholy and dismal place than even a dungeon could be, he had no idea of the perfect beauties of the possessions which his bountiful Creator had bestowed on him on earth; he had never experienced the delight of feeling himself the master of such a place. My whole mind was in a joyful and yet painful state of excitement, when I considered the unhappy situation of this excellent man; for it was only when I actually saw what he had possessed, that I could understand what he had lost.

"Oh, how beautiful it is here!" said Bob, also touched by the charm of the scene, though he could not form any idea of the reason for which this spot was doubly beautiful and precious to me.

"Wonderful! beautiful! glorious!" were the only words I could utter.

After we had thoroughly enjoyed the cool shade, and delighted ourselves with the wonderful beauty of the wood, we again trotted on for another half-hour in silence, while I thought, "If he were in my place, what would be his feelings to find himself once more on his own property!"

"There it is!—there it is!" suddenly cried out my young companion.

"What is there?" I asked, so strangely roused from my reflections—"What is there?" And I pulled up my horse.

"The castle—the castle—Dunsdale Castle! Look at the high tower, with its battlements peeping over the trees, and the bright windows in which the sun is reflected."

THE MADMAN OF ST. JAMES'.

"It is, it is, my boy! and now forward as fast as the horses can go," I cried, in as joyful a state of excitement as the young boy at my side; and giving our horses their heads, we dashed through the wood, as if engaged in a wild chase, or as if with pointed lance we would unhorse a flying enemy; and we did not slacken our speed until we saw the long-wished-for Castle of Dunsdale lying just before us.

It was a beautiful, charming, delightful scene. The wood opened gradually, and enclosed in a dark broad arch a large green space, in the middle of which, on a slightly-elevated lawn, stood the noble castle of the Viscount of Dunsdale. For some time we stopped, lost in admiration, and I drew a deep breath at the joyful consciousness of having reached the *first* object of my pilgrimage.

The castle, apparently newly built, or at all events recently restored externally, shone in the warm morning sunshine like a star amidst the surrounding foliage. It was built in the beautiful old German style, with its many ornamented pointed towers, richly-decorated windows, and high battlements, which had that friendly and protecting appearance peculiar to this solid and princely style of architecture. Only the bare flagstaff, which was erected on its highest point, showed that the owner of this beautiful castle was absent, as well as the stillness which reigned around proved that the happy sight of

VOL. II.
I

114 THE MADMAN OF ST. JAMES'.

cheerful faces, such as should often be seen in such places, was never seen here.

" Well, Bob, how do you like it ?" I asked in a cheerful voice.

" Ah, it is beautiful, sir ! you are quite right— but there, there !—as true as I live there are Mr. Graham's two little ponies feeding—I know them, I know them : that is Dick, and that is Harry—I know them well enough !"

And, sure enough, on the beautiful lawn before the castle were two small brown ponies. I could almost hear the beatings of my own heart, and involuntarily laid my hand upon it, when I saw thus before me, as Bob had said, the ponies which had belonged to Mr. Graham, the father of Ellinor, and which had also played a part in the melancholy events which I was endeavouring to unravel.

How long I might have reflected thus I do not know, had not Bob pointed out to me a man, who, bending down over one of the many shrubs, appeared to be occupied in tending the flowers, which in well-filled beds ornamented the rising lawn, on the top of which stood the noble castle itself.

" Go, Bob, and ring the bell," said I ; and the boy rode round to the iron railing which, ornamented with gilded points, surrounded the whole, and there, just before us, was a bell attached to the very handsome entrance door. The clear tones of the bell vibrated on the air, and an old man, who had been occupied with his flowers came up himself directly he heard it to inquire what we wanted.

At this moment I also approached the doorway; the man was speaking to Bob, but the distance prevented me from understanding what he said, for his voice was low and weakened by age. I saw, however, that he held his hands above his eyes in order to keep off the rays of the sun which dazzled him, and how, suddenly uttering a cry, he threw open the gate, and exclaimed with indescribable joy,—

" God be merciful to me! why that is my master's horse; come in, sir! come in! you bring me news of Lord Percy, or I cannot believe my eyes."

We sprang from our horses; the old man shook us heartily by the hand, as if we were dear old friends; and now only did I completely understand the purpose Percy might have had in view in offering me his horse, which, without its being necessary for me to speak a single word, immediately announced me as his friend, if I should anywhere meet with those who were acquainted with him.

Hardly, however, were we inside the gate—in fact, it had not yet closed behind us—when the old man, as quickly as he could, ran up the marble steps which led from the slope to the castle, and, disappearing through a side door, pulled violently at a large bell, whose sonorous tones summoned immediately several servants, to whom he hastily gave some hurried directions.

116   THE MADMAN OF ST. JAMES'.

They came round us, and stared at us; no one seemed to know exactly what was to be done or said first.

At last we followed the old man, who, with words of welcome, walked before us up the broad steps of the terrace, where he opened a large folding door, and ushered us into a semi-circular hall, ornamented with beautiful sculptures.

We were in the castle of Percy Viscount of Dunsdale.

"Here, sir, here," said I, taking Percy's letter to his steward out of my pocket-book, "are you the person to whom this letter is addressed, as I imagine you must be from the description the Viscount of Dunsdale gave me of you—are you Mr. Trollope?"

"Yes, sir, I am he."

"Well, then, read this letter, that you may feel quite sure I come from him whom you seem to love so much;—read, and convince yourself thoroughly of all that it is necessary for you to know."

"Yes, sir, yes!" cried the old man, still in his excited and tremulous voice; "he lives then—is not dead—not lost, eh? Did I not always say it?"

"Yes, he lives indeed, my old friend," I replied, "and lives in perfect health, and still more, with the intention of soon, very soon, being here again; but read, read; that letter contains it all."

The old man read the letter attentively, and with a

THE MADMAN OF ST. JAMES'.

delight which beamed in every feature of his honest face, and while he read, he kept exclaiming,—

" Yes, yes, it is he indeed ; and he still lives—is not dead—he will come again. Ah! that is wonderful! And you, sir, you are to see everything, and to have everything! Yes, yes, of course."

" Yes, sir," he continued, when he had finished reading it; " he *will* come here, and God will bless me, by letting me see him again. How I have prayed for him! Ah, sir!" sobbed the old man, as the bright tears ran down his withered cheeks, " I have been many long years in my master's family; I have gone through very much since I lived in it; and, believe me, sir, I have been very unhappy about my master. I loved him so! Ah, I knew the child, the boy, the youth, Percy, just as I knew his dear, good, beautiful mother. What kind of man must he have grown up!—a head taller than the rest of his family, perhaps! and such a form! such a face! and such a heart! But, that you may see in what good order I have kept everything during his long absence, and how I have managed, do, sir, come directly, and examine it all, and then we will sit down and talk, talk the whole night through. The old cellar-door shall turn once more on its hinges, and the new smoke-jack shall take its first turn, and in the empty, dismal stoves the bright flames shall burn again."

" But, my friend," I interrupted him, " we are now in the month of July!" I could not conceal the deep emotion which I felt at the sight of this joy, this devotion, this delight. Here again I was made to feel what an awful lot it was for Percy to be obliged for four years to live in a madhouse, among strangers, sick people, and lunatics, when in his own home such love and faithful devotion, such perfect enjoyment of life, awaited him on all sides. Just Heaven!

But I had no time to fall again into such reflections; the old man drew me, almost by force, through all the beautiful rooms of the castle, the grand saloons, the usual sitting rooms, the reception rooms, the library, and many more that he showed and named to me.

And how well kept were all those rich and splendid apartments! The gilded picture-frames of the old family portraits, as well as those of the modern paintings, were all bright and glistening; the velvet hangings as fresh, the thick, silken curtains as gracefully and delicately arranged, as if all had been finished but yesterday, and the large and brilliant mirrors as bright and clear as possible.

" How delighted Lord Percy will be to see all this again, to occupy these apartments, and to thank you for all your care," I said.

" Thank me, sir! what are you thinking of? He thank us? Why, we have done nothing more than our duty? Only let him come—only come—nothing more than come, with his beautiful wife! and the joy *that* will be to us will be reward enough for all we have done."

THE MADMAN OF ST. JAMES'. 119

After we had wandered through all the habitable apartments of the castle, and I had got through all my eulogiums, which were indeed sincere, for I found everything in the most perfect order, Mr. Trollope conducted me into the garden and the park, where the choicest and most beautiful trees and flowers were in the greatest perfection; finally, we went into the coach-houses and stables, many of the horses in which had belonged to the father of the late Lady Seymour.

Besides some splendid race-horses, I saw there six or eight beautiful, strong draught horses, which, added to the sight of a lightly-built hunting *calêche*, suggested to my mind a new idea, to which I shall have occasion to refer later.

After we had minutely examined all these places, and I had heard every particular concerning them from my delighted conductor, we returned to the dining-room of the castle, where the good steward introduced me to his wife, Mrs. Trollope, who during our absence had put on her best gown. She was a stout, elderly woman, of a phlegmatic disposition, but without the tiresome love of talking which many of her class possess. She was, however, troubled with a bad memory, and fits of absence of mind, which often made her speeches very tedious, and her recollections of the events she wished to talk about very uncertain. Thus the pleasure she felt at seeing a friend of her long absent master, and hearing news of him, was of a much calmer and more tranquil cha-

120   THE MADMAN OF ST. JAMES'.

racter than that of her good husband, but perfectly well corresponded with her disposition.

After she had bid me welcome, and I had given her the assurance of the pleasure it gave me to make her acquaintance, she asked me if I wished to dine directly, or if I would prefer to name a later hour; but as the morning's ride had not a little added to my appetite, I was very glad to hear that dinner would soon be ready; and at my request that she would favour me with her company at dinner, I received the answer that I was very kind, and that she certainly would not fail to obey my orders. Accordingly, the dinner-bell soon sounded, and we seated ourselves at the table. The dinner, although I was an unexpected guest, was well arranged, and I had the opportunity of observing that the wine in the long-closed cellar was not at all spoiled, and that the new smoke-jack was capable of doing as much good service as ever the old one could have done.

"Have you arranged all the papers and accounts?" I asked the steward, during dinner, "so that we may soon finish our business affairs?"

"All is ready for your inspection, sir; all the papers are in the iron chest in my room," answered Mr Trollope.

When the wine and dessert had been placed on the table, the old man could no longer restrain his curiosity, and asked me so many searching questions about his absent master that I saw myself obliged to tell him all that I had previously arranged to communicate respecting the Viscount of Dunsdale.

"You have certainly heard through Phillips, his Lordship's servant," I began, "that it was his intention to come here with his young wife?"

"Yes, sir, yes, he told me that."

"Well, then, you know also that, by his non-appearance, his journey and his intentions were interrupted, and that by circumstances which I am not at liberty to name to you fully, but which most likely you will understand better one day."

"Yes, sir; that was what we expected."

"Well, through unfortunate and unforeseen circumstances, unlooked and unwished for on both sides, a separation of Lord Percy and his wife was necessary, the duration of which was uncertain."

"Hem! Yes, sir, *that* I believe also."

"Through this sudden and hasty separation, which, as already said, did not rest with them——"

"I understand, sir."

"An unexpected circumstance took place which obliged Lord Percy to undertake a long journey abroad; and he could not give his wife any positive information of his place of residence, while she remained in England, travelling about from one place to another, and waiting with the greatest anxiety the return of the viscount."

"Well, and where is she now?"

"Yes, that is just the question which no one can

answer, and which I was just going to ask you, for I thought perhaps she might have come here and awaited the arrival of his lordship, who is just now, at last, on the point of returning to Dunsdale Castle."

The steward, who had drunk a glass or two of good old wine, looked at me and his wife somewhat crest-fallen, as if there was a share of blame attaching to him that his master's wife was absent.

"No, sir, no!" he stammered, very much embarrassed; "she has never been here."

"That is a difficult point, a most vexatious point," I answered; "and there is nothing left for us, as most likely all her letters are lost, but to believe that she has gone to some of her relations, who live at a great distance from this place, and will remain with them until further news, or——"

"But who, or where are these relations of hers?"

This question was rather a difficult one for me: I must either tell the truth or a falsehood, but neither of these would I do. I therefore evaded it by resuming,—

"Or, that Lady Dunsdale is travelling after her husband, and perhaps arrives just at the place he has already left; and, as I was of opinion that if she were not here herself, she would, under any circumstances, send here tidings of herself, I wished and hoped to gain some information concerning her of you."

"Ah, indeed, sir! No. That, indeed, is very

vexatious. Nobody sent me any tidings. I know nothing about her."

"Stop, dear husband; and you, sir, pray excuse me," interrupted his wife, in her calmest voice; "but just now something occurs to me. It might be about six weeks ago, it was, I really believe, the day you rode over to Farmer Thompson's——"

"That was seven weeks ago."

"Well, then, seven weeks ago it was, at—it was in the afternoon—at about four o'clock——"

"Five o'clock, if you like," hastily observed the husband—"five o'clock, if you like; only do please go on."

"That a carriage drove up, in which were seated a young lady and an old gentleman, who came to make some inquiries respecting the Viscount of Dunsdale."

"What?" exclaimed I and Mr. Trollope in one breath. "And you never told me a word about it?" added he.

"I forgot it, my dear,—I forgot it; there is always so much to do here."

"And was nobody else present when they came?"

"Not a soul, my love; I was just standing at the gateway."

"But how, and with whom did she come, and where from?" I asked, as quickly as I could utter the words, for it struck me at once who it might be.

"As I said, sir, she came in a carriage with an old gentleman, and they were coming from——"

124   THE MADMAN OF ST. JAMES'.

"And did she mention no name?"

"Not that I remember, sir."

"But what was she like? And what did she ask about?"

"Ah, sir, she was very pretty—yes, very pretty, although she looked rather pale and sorrowful. She asked if his lordship was at Dunsdale. And when I told her that for four years he had not been here, nor had we heard a word about him, she sighed, and gave me—yes, that's right; I remember now—she gave me a letter."

"What! and I did not hear a word about it?" cried Mr. Trollope, extremely angry, dashing his dinner napkin down on the table.

"I forgot to tell you, my dear."

"To the devil with your forgetfulness; and now——"

"But where is the letter?" I anxiously inquired.

"Yes, sir, where the letter is? Ah! just wait—wait a little; I must try and remember. Yes, yes, I think it must be in my drawer."

And the forgetful woman went out to fetch the letter, while her husband, usually so peaceably disposed, sent her, as far as words could send her, many times to the devil.

After some time, however, during which Mr. Trollope had been rushing about the room in a state of great and angry excitement, whistling loudly sometimes for a change, she returned, and to our dismay told us that she really could not possibly find the letter anywhere, for she did not recollect for certain if she had put it into her drawers; it might be she had put it somewhere else, but some time or another she should certainly recollect where she had put it.

"How extraordinary!" I thought, "that six weeks ago Lady Ellinor should have been here, just at the very time I made Percy's acquaintance at St. James'. How wonderful are the ways of Providence! And do you know nothing more of the lady?" I asked. "Did she not say anything else?"

"No, sir, nothing; nothing at all. She gave me the letter, and they drove off."

"Did you not remark anything else about the lady?"

"No, sir, nothing; except, yes, that a large black dog sprang out of the carriage when it stopped. I remember that at first I was afraid of him, for he was as big as Minnie, our little black cow."

"It was she!—it was she! I was right," I exclaimed joyfully. "And where were they going? which direction did they take?"

"The road to London, sir."

"To London, indeed!" groaned out the old man sarcastically, looking angrily at his forgetful wife. "There are many places between Dunsdale Castle and London, confound you! And that just then I should not have been at home!"

"That was fate, my good friend," I remarked, and I began to reflect a little.

"London!" I thought, "that is something; the letter, I suppose, contained the rest. I will go to London too: without doubt she is gone to her uncle, Sir William Graham; and her father was with her—well, that, at least, is something to know."

"So you are certain it was she, sir?" asked the old man, somewhat cooler, and seeing that I did not appear to be so very discontented.

"I am perfectly sure it was the Lady Ellinor, Lord Percy's wife, for whom Lord Percy and I are searching, and whom nobody can find. For Heaven's sake, do try once more to find that letter, Mrs. Trollope; it is of the greatest importance."

She promised she would, and again retired to resume her search.

"And now one more question, my dear Mr. Trollope. Have you heard anything lately of his lordship's father, the Marquis of Seymour?"

"Nothing, sir, nothing at all since the sudden disappearance of his eldest son Percy, your friend and my dear master. The last news I heard was from that extraordinary paragraph in the newspaper. You know about it, perhaps?"

"Indeed I do. Well?"

"It was a statement which certainly grieved me very much; but, if I might be allowed to say what I think, I should say it was as false as anything could

THE MADMAN OF ST. JAMES'. 127

possibly be. If I were my Lord Percy, I would—
oh, I do not know what I would not do. But ——"

"How false?" I asked, "for they went to law
about it, eh?"

"Nevertheless it is a confounded falsehood, in spite
of all the legal tricks and stratagems to which they
may have resorted, and I know one who can prove
the real truth, and that one is myself! Yes, sir,
I myself was present at the marriage, although
perhaps nobody thought of that; for it is nearly nine-
and-twenty years ago. And that stupid woman, my
wife, was there also, although I dare say she has
forgotten all about it long since."

"I am glad you have told me this," I said. "I
shall not forget it."

And indeed I was very glad to have thus found a
witness; they had therefore *not* all disappeared from
the face of the earth, as even Percy himself seemed
inclined to believe.

"But continue, my good old friend."

"Well, sir, the news did certainly grieve me very
much, for I was an old servant of the noble family of
Dunsdale. But when I saw my Lord Percy succeed
to his rights here as eldest child and heir of this
family, I did not care so much about the property
and estates of the Seymours for him; for Lord Percy
would be rich enough with his mother's fortune,
without getting anything from his father's, although,
of course, it legally belongs to him. But who knows

if Lord Percy would have been as happy with the property of his father as he is sure of being with that of his mother and grandfather?"

"How so? For even more than enough in the way of money would not hurt a reasonable man, I should think."

"Yes, sir, it may be as you say, but then again it may not. May God forgive Lord Seymour all his sins, as I trust He will pardon all mine; but I should think there was some difference in property as to from whom it was inherited and how obtained. But with respect to Lady Seymour—God bless her!—she has forgiven him, I am sure; but there is a higher Judge above us, as you well know."

This "as you well know" from the old man seemed to refer more to the occurrences between the Marquis of Seymour and his wife than to the higher Judge above us, and was a hint for me to leave off my inquiries in this direction with respect to him; for Mr. Trollope seemed to imagine that I was acquainted with all that he knew himself. It would certainly have been no difficult task to have obtained from him a clear insight into many events, with which at present I was but imperfectly acquainted, for he dropped many hints about them; but I felt no inclination to intrude into secrets which Percy himself had veiled in silence, or had appeared as if he himself knew little about. I was therefore silent after the steward's last remark, and he seemed also to have come to an end with the outpourings of his honest heart. We rose from the table.

From the dining-room we proceeded to Mr. Trollope's private sitting-room, for I longed to examine the papers of the viscount, as I still cherished some indefinite hope that I might find some tidings of Ellinor among them.

The old steward was right in saying that everything was in the best order, for I found it to be the case even in the most trifling matters. First, he placed before me the endorsements of the notary in London for bills and moneys which he had receipted and received in the name of his master; then came the accounts of money paid by the farmers, and these also, were quite correct. The money sent by the notary was in paper, as was also most of the money received from the farmers; but there was also some gold. As I had arranged with Percy, I took the gold and part of the paper-money, and drew up a statement of how much I had found, and how much I had taken away. I gave the old steward a copy of this statement, and then caused the chest to be restored to its place of safety, under lock and key.

But it was a great labour to read through all the letters which had arrived. I took them up to my room, and spent nearly all the afternoon and evening in their perusal. I immediately looked for those addressed by a female hand, but not one was there. The most of them I found to be merely friendly

VOL. II.   K

130   THE MADMAN OF ST. JAMES'.

letters from all parts ; but not one of them contained
a word which related in the least degree to the circumstances which occasioned my present journey.

I had nearly gone through them all, when, with
the greatest anxiety and joy, I observed a little note,
written on the finest paper, and I hastily broke the
seal; but all my joy vanished when I had finished
reading it.

This letter was, indeed, from Ellinor, although
dated a year back, from a little village on the road
from Dunsdale to London, and contained the following lines, word for word :—

" MY BELOVED PERCY,—

"God alone knows if this letter, as well as
others I have written to you, will ever reach your
hands; and although I must almost doubt this, yet I
shall never be weary of following you with my wishes
and my blessings, though even on earth they may
never reach you ; but my heart tells me that you still
live; for, without this hope, how could it still beat?
But that you are *compelled* to be silent, as well as
absent from your Ellinor, is proved by the sorrowful
fact that I hear nothing of you. If you were at
liberty, and able to follow the dictates of your heart,
I am certain nothing would prevent you from searching for me by letter as well as in person. May it
please God to spare my life, at least long enough
to know you are happy ; for myself, I have no

other wish than that! A barrier has been raised between us which is not to be surmounted. Ah! that the curse of such a father should have been sanctioned by heaven.

"I send this letter to Dunsdale Castle; there you will most likely go first when you are again at liberty, and there, at least, the hatred of those who have stepped between our love is less able to pursue us.

"We are going—that is, I and my father, who greets you affectionately—to Sir William Graham, my uncle, in London, who has given up his profession, and requires our care. There you will certainly find me; and should any change take place in our plans, intelligence shall always be sent to Dunsdale Castle.

"Farewell, my only and ever-beloved one! If even my heart is breaking with anxiety, may God still keep me faithful and resigned.—Your

"ELLINOR."

Two points struck me while reading this beautiful letter. First, it appeared to me somewhat reserved, and then the writer repeatedly alluded to the state of her health, which was not at all satisfactory.

The first might have been caused by having written so often, and in vain; the second gave me an insight into the forbearing and loving heart of Ellinor, who wished to conceal from Percy that she suffered. That she suffered, and in no slight degree, of that I felt quite sure. "May it please God to spare my life—at least, long enough," &c.; and, "if even my heart is breaking, may God keep me faithful!" These words inspired me with serious anxiety for this precious life, for they appeared to me to conceal the existence of a deep-rooted bodily ailment.

And now? She mentions going to London and remaining there; and should they change their residence, they would send news of it directly to Dunsdale Castle; and now six weeks ago she had herself been here, and with her own hands had left a letter. Now, could this letter contain the news she had promised? and had they really changed their place of residence? and where was this letter which she had brought thus herself? The success of my whole undertaking depended on this.

It was sought for, but it could not be found. Nearly the whole of the following day we occupied ourselves in seeking for it. We ransacked the rooms of the steward, but no letter! Fatigued by the continual anxiety which this vexatious affair and our fruitless search for this important letter produced, and angry with the old forgetful Mrs. Trollope, who alone had been the cause of this annoyance, and, finally, full of anxiety about the fate of Ellinor, I spent the last few hours of my stay in Dunsdale Castle in a state of great irritation as well as anxiety.

THE MADMAN OF ST. JAMES'. 133

Ill at ease, vexed, without anything particular to do, when everybody knows that occupation is the best remedy under such circumstances, the third morning after my arrival I determined to recommence my journey, previously giving the steward the necessary directions respecting his future arrangements.

"My dear Mr. Trollope," said I to him, "one circumstance in Dunsdale Castle pleases me very much, and there is another which grieves me. I have found everything in the most perfect order, just as Lord Percy told me it would be, and expected from your care: *that* has pleased me. But that I have not succeeded in the object I had in view besides in coming here, and have been greatly perplexed in my endeavours to find Lord Percy's wife, *that* has much vexed me."

"Ah, yes, sir! you mean the lost letter?"

"Yes, I do; and the loss of such a letter, in every way so important for me and my whole undertaking, is the very worst thing which could have happened; my hopes depended on it, and that is the reason why I do not leave so well satisfied as I hoped to be when I came here. Spare no time and no trouble in seeking for that letter, and should you be lucky enough to find it, send it to me directly by a trusty messenger— by a messenger, recollect, not by the post, otherwise it might miss me again. Send it to Codrington Hall,

134 THE MADMAN OF ST. JAMES'.

to which place I shall go first, and should it not find me there, then send it on to the address I shall leave with the steward at Codrington Hall.

I took these precautions, for I did not know for certain if I should find the Marquis of Seymour at Codrington, nor how long I should be obliged to remain with him; that is to say, if he wished me to remain with him at all. If, however, I did not find him there, I was determined to travel after him, wherever he might happen to be.

"Are you sure that you have perfectly understood me, Mr. Trollope?" I asked.

"Yes, sir—first to Codrington Hall—every thing shall be attended to as you desire."

"But you must also be mindful of any news which may arrive here; it might be that letters were brought here again."

"Do not be uneasy, sir, and do not mistrust me; no more letters shall be brought here or taken in without my knowledge."

"And when a carriage happens to drive up——"

"Ah! I understand—do not be uneasy; the devil of forgetfulness shall not play his pranks here again."

"And all fresh letters, too, are to be sent after me; if necessary by another messenger."

"'Certainly, sir; to be sure; I know my duty."

"And now, in the second place, hold yourself in readiness to execute at a moment's notice any orders I may send you in his lordship's name; for it might happen that I gave you orders to send me im-

THE MADMAN OF ST. JAMES'. 135

mediately a carriage and horses to some place I might mention; do not hesitate an instant—every moment is precious to him and to me. All that now appears to you perplexing in these extraordinary proceedings shall one day be explained to you. And now, my good Mr. Trollope, let my horses be brought round immediately, and then farewell!"

The good old man spoke a few words in reply, and then retired to see that my orders were executed.

With respect to the way in which I should travel forward, I had hesitated a few moments if it would not have been desirable for me to have taken the hunting *calèche* with four of Percy's horses, to dash on as fast and as far as possible, and then to proceed with post horses. Without doubt this mode of travelling would have been more convenient, and would have brought me more quickly to the places I wished to visit. But, with respect to my own convenience, I did not feel in the slightest degree disposed to consult that, if by the sacrifice of all my personal comfort I could be of the least service to Percy; so that consideration for myself formed no part of my calculation; but the quickness of my journey was another affair. Yes! I should travel more quickly, but should I, after all, derive much benefit from it? I think not. Could I, sitting in a carriage, and travelling on the usual high roads, make those inquiries I deemed it necessary to make, stop where I wished, and follow at once all the trifling clues I might obtain? Certainly not. On horseback I could travel slowly or quickly, in a word, just as circumstances required. I could stop, wait, make inquiries; yes, turn back when and where I liked, or as it seemed to be advisable. Besides, Percy himself—and this it was which decided me—had arranged my mode of travelling, and I was perfectly certain he must have had good reasons for it. If, when travelling in a carriage, my undertaking should be unsuccessful, he might reproach me that I had deviated from the given path; were I unsuccessful on horseback, I only acted on his own wishes. Nevertheless, if prudence or necessity had made it urgent, I should most decidedly have changed my mode of travelling; but for the present this was not the case, although later it might be.

Acting on these good reasons, I decided unhesitatingly upon continuing my journey as I had begun it, and this determination I carried out, and the future will prove that it was successful.

The horses, well fed and well groomed, were brought out. We mounted, and amidst the blessings and good wishes of the assembled household, on a Sunday morning I rode away, with my good Bob, from Dunsdale Castle.

We first took the road to London, but I left it again, after a few hours, to travel in the direction of Codrington Hall; for this was to be the next, and certainly not the most pleasant object of my present journey.

CHAPTER VII.

RESEARCHES.

BETWEEN Codrington Hall and Dunsdale Castle I had about seventy miles before me, and these I determined to get over in three days, which was no great work for our good horses.

The road conducted us first through a wood, which, although not so beautiful as the one we had passed through to Dunsdale Castle, still proved shady and pleasant enough.

Occupied with my own thoughts on the present state of things, I paid but little attention to what my companion was doing; it was only after we had ridden on in silence for some miles, that I looked round for him, for it had just occurred to me that he was not riding by my side as usual.

" Where are you, Bob?" I called out, and I found he was riding behind me, eating the breakfast he had brought with him from the castle.

" Here, sir!" he replied, trotting up quickly to my side. "I would not disturb you, for you seemed to be deep in thought."

138 THE MADMAN OF ST. JAMES'.

" That does not signify; you can always ride by me. Go on eating; do you like it?"

" Yes, sir; it is excellent—excellent. In the morning it always tastes best."

" Well, and afternoon and evening your appetite does not fail you either."

" No, sir; no. There were such good things to be had at the castle!—never in my life did I taste any things like them."

" Well, you have not eaten much yet, to what you may, perhaps, if——"

" Yes—hem! I should like to have remained there a few days longer—at least, just the Sunday."

" You may go back, Bob, and come after me in a few days, if you like. I will allow you."

The boy looked at me very earnestly, put his breakfast into his pocket, and answered,—

" No, sir; I did not mean it like that. I only thought it would be very nice to have just such a life as Mr. Trollope, the steward, leads yonder."

" Well, you may live long enough to have that wish fulfilled one day," said I, meaning to cheer Bob, who appeared to be a little embarrassed and hurt by my former hasty words.

" Ah, sir, that is just what I should like— that is just the place I should like to have!"

I reflected for a few moments, and then repeated, " That is not such an improbable wish, after all, and

THE MADMAN OF ST. JAMES'. 139

may one day be fulfilled. Yes, yes," I continued, as he smiled doubtingly; "your father, at least, is sure of the place, and you are young, and may succeed him."

"But Lord Percy must be here again before that happens."

"Ah," thought I, "the boy is right!—that is true." And we then went on for some time without speaking.

The morning was warm, but towards noon it became quite sultry, and during the hottest part of the day we rested two hours longer than usual. Towards evening we found ourselves out of the county of Dunsdale, and the next morning reached a spot which bore quite a different appearance from the rest of the country we had passed through. Low fir-trees covered the ground to a great extent; then came half-cultivated land; then again a plantation of fir-trees, and at last an extensive moor.

"It is not so beautiful anywhere as at Dunsdale, sir. Ah, that large beautiful forest, and the fresh lawn;—if we could but go back there again!"

"The world is large, Bob, and there are many places in it far more beautiful than Dunsdale. Nevertheless, you are right; it *is* beautiful there, and I too like to remain at a place that pleases me; but now we have got other business in hand, and must ride on without looking back. To-morrow you will be with your aunt Ursula."

140   THE MADMAN OF ST. JAMES'.

"Ah, Aunt Ursula! what will she say to see me ride up on horseback?"

"Yes, and how pleased she will be! How long is it since you last saw her?"

"I have not seen her for three months, sir."

"Not for three months!" I thought, "and the boy already longs for his home and relations. Percy has been obliged to leave much more, and has been already four long years away and—where?"

And we rode on again until the evening approached, and we found a lodging for the second night.

Early the third morning found us ready to begin our journey again. Bob's heart beat high with joy, and mine with expectation. I was soon to see Codrington Hall, Mr. Graham's quiet dwelling by the lake, and make the acquaintance of the Marquis of Seymour. Sweet and bitter feelings by turn took possession of my heart, and with feverish impatience I trotted on more quickly than before.

The afternoon came; we reached a green wood, which could be crossed by several paths. The farther we went, the more silent we both became, although from very different causes. The boy looked to the right, then to the left; suddenly he stopped his horse, touched my arm, and cried out,—

"Here—here, stop, sir!—here at last are the two well-known roads,—this one to the right leads to my aunt's house, this one to the left to Codrington Hall—

THE MADMAN OF ST. JAMES'.   141

just to the very spot where Mr. Graham's house stands. You cannot miss it, sir!"

I understood what the boy meant by these words. I stood still, and looked around me.

"Very well, Bob!" said I with a peculiar feeling of oppression; "go to your aunt, remember me to her, and enjoy the happiness of seeing her again. When, however, you have told her all you have got to say, come early to-morrow morning to Codrington Hall, where I think of remaining to-night. Take good care of your horse, and now, good-bye until to-morrow."

The boy took off his little cap, bowed, and said, " I wish you good luck, sir!—greet the ' black man,' Seymour, from his best rabbit-hunter. Good-bye, sir, good-bye!" and calling this out with a cheerful laugh, which, however, was quite respectful and good-humoured, he gave spur to his spirited little pony, and dashed towards his aunt's dwelling, for he wished to appear before her in good style on horseback, and as grand as any gentleman.

I stood still until I could see him no longer, and then, without taking notice of anything around me, I rode slowly onwards.

Once more I was alone with my own thoughts, and these thoughts engrossed me entirely, as such intense and anxious thoughts are sure to do when once they take possession of the mind. I was now, then, not far from the place which had been the scene of so much

142   THE MADMAN OF ST. JAMES'.

happiness and so much sorrow. How should I find it? What ideas would the sight of it convey to my mind? for even inanimate objects over which the storm of life has swept, and upon which the sun of happiness has once shone, have their own language; and this language is the more distinct and comprehensible as it speaks not to our ears only, but to our eyes, and to our hearts.

I was gradually awakened from the dreamy state into which I had fallen while approaching Mr. Graham's house, by the extraordinary movements of my horse: at first I did not heed them, and only became aware of them when they affected me personally.

Gradually the animal had passed from his usual quiet pace into a gentle trot, had pricked up his ears, snuffed the air, and even neighed aloud, throwing his head up repeatedly, as if with pride and pleasure. Without any guiding on my part, this trot changed into a sort of gallop, which gradually became swifter and swifter, until I could no longer restrain his speed. I looked round, in order to ascertain if any thing had startled him, but I could see nothing.

Suddenly it occurred to me, could this be the animal's instinct? Could he have recognized the formerly well-known path, or could they have brought to his mind old recollections? Yes, it could not be otherwise. Bravour had recognized the road, and the goal to which it led; and to reach the end of

THE MADMAN OF ST. JAMES'.

his journey sooner, he had accelerated his speed, and his neighing was a greeting to the well-known locality.

"Aha!" thought I, "Bravour knows where he is going to; he has often travelled this road before, and knows it better than I do—so forward, my good friend!" I gave him his head, and he dashed on with me through the brushwood under the trees, so that it broke and rustled on all sides, and the black moorland was soon left far behind us.

I knew his safe paces even at this tearing speed; I was not at all timid; we dashed on, the horse snorted and seemed to fly—I was obliged to hold on my hat—see! here we come to the little stream —with one bound it is behind us. Ah! that was the stream over which he had so often carried Percy in happier days—a few more seconds and he stood still, snorting and neighing loudly before the closed doors of an old grey stone building which was supported on each side by a round tower overgrown with moss.

But no sound, no voice of welcome, answered Bravour's joyful neighing. I threw myself off, and let go my hold of the horse's bridle.

I knocked at the closed window shutters—all was still as in the dead of night. Yes, even the wood around seemed to be mourning with that house—all was so still. Not a bird chirped; not a leaf moved; such a deathlike silence pervaded that solitary place,

144   THE MADMAN OF ST. JAMES'.

that I shuddered at this loneliness, which was increased by my own imaginations.

Ah! how different do we generally find the places which we have pictured in our fancy! Seldom so beautiful, so animated, and cheerful; much oftener more bounded, more lonely, more forsaken, more sad.

A profound feeling of melancholy took possession of me, and almost overpowered me. The closed doors and windows of this forsaken dwelling seemed to me like the lifeless body of a beloved friend, whose eyes, shrouded in the gloom of night, are closed for ever to the cheerful light of day.

"Would it—could it be for ever?" whispered a sorrowful voice in the depth of my heart.

I could not answer; I heard nothing but the loud breathing and interrupted snorting of my horse, who was smelling round the cracks of the closed door, on the threshold of which a fair hand had often fed him delicately, and patted his arched neck.

I turned to the right. Ah! there lay that calm blue stream, winding far away, clear and peaceful like the soul of a slumbering child. Not a single angry wave cast its foam over the mossy shore, not a single breath ruffled those quiet waters gleaming in the sunshine.

Involuntarily I raised my eyes towards heaven. The sky was clear, pure, and bright as crystal: as far as I could see not one cloud was there. "Percy!"

I cried involuntarily, " thy fate is not yet fulfilled ; clouds and storm, waves and night are not over for thee yet ! "

How long I thus stood there lost in reflection I no longer know, but it must have been a very long time. I was aroused from it by the loud neighing of my horse who, perhaps, missed his accustomed welcome there ; and I found myself with my arms crossed on my breast, my eyes fixed on the cold stones before the door of the house, from which no one issued to bid me welcome.

Making a violent effort, I aroused myself from these dreams, and walked round the old building, examining every spot, every window, every part ; for all was important and of interest to me. Once I called aloud, for it seemed to me as if I heard some slight movement within the house, as if somebody was rousing up from a deep sleep ; but the sound was only imaginary, no voice answered ; the house too, like the wood, was silent, although formerly sounds enough might have been heard there both of joy and sorrow. I went again to the door to Bravour, took him by the bridle, and walked with him into the chestnut avenue, which had so often and so minutely been described to me.

I examined every tree : here, perhaps, had Ellinor reclined with Othello upon the grass, when one had approached her from the wood, blessed with that richest gift of nature, a pure warm heart, and that

VOL. II.   L

146   THE MADMAN OF ST. JAMES'.

heart full of love for her! When Percy drew near—
no, there—no, here—no, yonder—under that beech-
tree, perhaps, she was.

Dreams! dreams! Why do they so often visit
the slumbering soul of man, to torment, to goad, to
urge it on to bold deeds and daring undertakings?

But the dreams which hovered around me on this
particular day, at this hour, although, perhaps, tor-
menting, were not goading; they awoke in me no thirst
for action—I confess it openly—no, only a feeling of
sorrow, inconceivably deep, a heartfelt sorrow for
the lost happiness of these two excellent, noble, and
sorely-tried hearts.

I walked up the chestnut avenue; already from a
distance I had perceived the grey, ancient castle of
Lord Seymour, which looked as dark and desolate as
was the chilled heart of its proprietor. The infectious
gloom of the place made it resemble the dwelling of
a bad spirit, which had enchained that proud, un-
tameable, cold heart since its earliest youth.

I approached nearer; all warmth vanished from
my breast. I felt cold, although it was the middle
of summer, beneath the scorching rays of a July sun;
cold, icy cold, amidst the feelings of love and its
cherished memories.

At last I stood just before the door, where the man
with the grimly-smiling face had stood—where
Mortimer had stood, and witnessed the first loving
embrace of his brother and Ellinor, and had sworn to

be revenged for his lost happiness, and had kept his word.

All my melancholy suddenly vanished; I nerved myself; I felt again that I was not there to dream, but—to act. I sprang upon my horse, and rode quickly round the large building, until I came to the grand entrance.

But no favourable impression or feeling of welcome did it give me; cold as those who dwelt there, whose chilled hearts were only animated when moved by the heat of passion, was the appearance of this deserted looking dwelling. It was built of hard, dark-coloured freestone, and was at this moment almost uninhabited.

A large, broad, heavy-looking terrace, built of the same stone, sprang from the middle of the building, and terminated in a flight of steps. Upon the terrace stood eight old, half-withered orange trees, with yellow, dried-up leaves, looking in their way quite as forlorn and solitary as the rest of the place. Not a flower, not a friendly blooming shrub, was to be seen; no verdant lawn or cultivated enclosure; only withered grass and stone, damp moss and grey earth,—that was all I saw there. I rode along the terrace, and looked about for somebody to speak to—all was as quiet as death. By a loud shout I was just going to give a sign of my presence, when I perceived the old rusty knocker on the door. I took hold of it, and knocked lustily, till its dull and

148 THE MADMAN OF ST. JAMES'.

hollow sounds could be heard through the neighbourhood, and awoke the echoes of the deserted
wood.

At last I heard some one from within approaching
the door, and after a little while an insolent-looking
man appeared at the threshold, and stared at me, as
if he expected to see anything rather than a human
being before this inhospitable-looking house.

" What do you want?" he asked roughly.

" Like master, like man!" thought I, and answered,—

" Is this Codrington Hall, the seat of the Marquis
of Seymour?"

" It is; and what do you want with him?"

" To speak to him. Is he at home?"

" No."

" Where is he, then?"

" Three days ago he went to London; he is ill, and
is gone there for medical advice."

" Do you know when he will return? Did he
leave no orders behind?"

" I know nothing about it; when he is well, and
when he likes, he will come back, I suppose."

" Then you are of the same opinion as I am. Is
any of his family here?"

The man stared at me, as it appeared, with
astonishment, and answered,—

" No one, sir! Lord Mortimer went to London
also."

THE MADMAN OF ST. JAMES'. 149

" Three days ago?"

" Why, I have told you so already; yes, three days ago."

" You don't seem to know yet that that which is heard for the second time is better understood; remember that for the future. Which road did his lordship take?"

" That one there," pointing with his finger towards the wood. I turned round towards that direction, and looked at it for a moment in silence. By the time, however, I turned round again, the ruffian had almost closed the door.

" Very well," said I, and was just going away.

"Will you leave any message?" asked the man hesitatingly, half opening the door again, at the sight of my not very pleased-looking face.

I reflected a moment. At last an idea occurred to me; to this day I do not know how it passed my lips, but it served to punish the man later for his rudeness, as the reader will know at the right time.

" *A greeting from St. James'!* you can say."

" St. James'?—very well."

" Good afternoon!"

" Good afternoon, sir!" and with a loud bang the man closed the door.

" To London!" said I to myself; "well, I suppose then I *am* to go to London. Well! Ellinor is perhaps there also; so there will not only be the night, but day also on my path."

150   THE MADMAN OF ST. JAMES'.

Once more I turned Bravour's head towards the chestnut avenue; he appeared better pleased to leave the house than to come to it. He neighed again as we passed Mr. Graham's former dwelling. Once more I looked at the deserted habitation; once more I looked at the stream, and then, sorry as I was to be thus obliged to tax the strength of the good horse, I quickly retraced the road we had come, and rode on towards the house of the pedlar's sister, for I longed to feel myself once more among human beings.

The evening had already begun when I dismounted before the cottage, which I found without any difficulty. I knocked at the first door on the right hand, where I heard some one speaking, and on entering I found Aunt Ursula, with her nephew Bob, sitting most comfortably at table, enjoying their supper.

Both looked at me with astonishment, as with a friendly bow I thus suddenly stood before them; and both immediately rose from their seats.

"You receive more guests this evening than you had any reason to expect this morning, Mrs. Dickstone," said I; "but necessity compels me to burden you with my company;" and with these words I offered her my hand, as she had kindly extended hers, as soon as Bob, by the exclamation of my name, had made known to her that it was his present master who had just entered the room.

THE MADMAN OF ST. JAMES'. 151

"Although your unexpected appearance surprises me, sir," she answered, "I am very glad to see you, and to be able to express to you my thanks for your kindness to my nephew. But I am surprised that they did not detain you at Codrington Hall, as I hear it was your intention to remain the night there.

"'Man proposes and God disposes,' my good woman! It was certainly my intention to remain there, but you will remember that a few years since another guest claimed your hospitality, one who had a far greater right to stay at Codrington Hall than I have, and who yet preferred to occupy your quiet rooms to yonder magnificent saloons. Besides, three days ago Lord Seymour left for London, and I felt no particular inclination to stop with his rude servants, even if they had asked me to remain."

"Ah! that is it; then be pleased to sit down, sir, and partake of what we have. To-day is a happy day for me, for my good Bob is here again!"

Bob was delighted at the joy of his aunt, placed a chair for me at the table, upon which plates, and all that was necessary, were soon arranged, and without any ceremony I sat down and made myself comfortable.

"I hear," resumed Mrs. Dickstone, "that you are travelling on business for Lord Percy, sir; and as I have been waiting in vain for my brother, who also stands in connection with his lordship, and who never

152   THE MADMAN OF ST. JAMES'.

left me any direction where I might find him, I am particularly glad to see you, because I have got a letter for him."

" A letter ?" I exclaimed; " where is it ?"

Bob took it out of his pocket, in which he had already placed it, and handed it to me.

My conjecture was correct; it was another letter from Ellinor. Thus, she had sent news here also in the hope that a way might be found of letting Percy receive it. The letter was almost similar to the other, only it had the advantage of having been written but three months back, after Phillips had fetched his sons from his sister. From this letter, therefore, I had still more recent news of the writer, as her place of residence was here given in London, at the house of her uncle. But why had she, six weeks ago, undertaken another journey to Dunsdale, if her plans had remained the same? The reason of this journey appeared to me rather incomprehensible, if it were not that she hoped by personal inquiry to be more sure of success. If this were not the case, I was then convinced she had changed her place of residence, was therefore no longer in London, and that the letter, unfortunately delivered to Mrs. Trollope, was a notification of that change. With respect to Ellinor, therefore, I was not sure of finding her in London, but I was at least hopeful that I might obtain a clue from her uncle.

What also grieved me afresh was, that in this

letter also, although mentioned in the most tender, forbearing manner, allusion was again made to the suffering state of health of the writer. For a few moments I leaned back in my chair, deep in thought, and I added this new anxiety in my search to the many others with which my head was filled.

"Does the letter contain bad news, sir?"

"No, Mrs. Dickstone, not exactly bad news; on the contrary, it revives my hopes of finding Lady Dunsdale, who, as you most probably know, is not with her husband; but still I am rather anxious about the state of her health, although nothing positive concerning it is contained in this letter,"

"Oh! I hope there is nothing very much amiss; that would grieve me beyond anything. Yes, sir, I do indeed know what unhappy events took place at that time, even if I do not know where his lordship has been compelled to stop so long; for on this subject my brother has not said a word to anybody, not even to me. Ah! and perhaps she is suffering too, —that beautiful Miss Ellinor—that dear child."

"Tell me all you know about her. I have never seen her, and yet I like so much to hear about her."

And for some time the good woman kept on relating so many endearing and admirable things of Ellinor and her father, that I had hardly ears enough to listen, much less memory enough to remember them all.

Before we retired to rest, we arranged all that

154   THE MADMAN OF ST. JAMES'.

was to be done the following morning before we should begin our journey; we then talked about the journey itself, until at length my hostess conducted me to a chamber, which had originally been prepared for Bob, but was now for my use.

It was the same which Percy had occupied during his exile from his father's house; the same bare walls and low ceiling had sheltered him, and the same wild vine crept around the little window which had shaded him from the rays of the sun. In that chamber I passed a long and sleepless night.

Early the next morning we sent a messenger to Codrington Hall with a written request from me that they would forward any letter, which might possibly be sent there for me, by the same messenger who brought it, immediately to London; to which I added, enclosed and sealed, the address of Sir William Graham. I was obliged to take this step, sorry as I was to do it; for if the contents of this enclosed direction became known, the name of Sir William Graham might only cause suspicion, as well as supply the means to work against me.

But, in the first place, necessity required it; for there was no other means of receiving Ellinor's letter, which was more important than any thing else, in case it should be found. And then, after all, it did not much signify to me if suspicion arose against me or not. I was bound to act, and step out openly with my opinions, come what might. Return to Dunsdale Castle I really could not; for time was precious, and my own wishes urged me powerfully onwards towards some decision.

At the hour appointed for our departure, Bob led out the horses, which had been very comfortably groomed and fed, and after a farewell, particularly energetic on Bob's part, we sat once more in our saddles.

I did not forget to give Mrs. Dickstone the direction also, in case a letter should arrive, so that she might send it after me.

The journey which now lay before me was longer than any I had yet undertaken; for, on account of the horses, I wanted nearly nine days for it. All went on as well as I could possibly wish, with the exception that, notwithstanding all my endeavours and inquiries, I could nowhere discover the least trace of Ellinor.

However, not to tire the reader, who will readily excuse a more detailed description of this long ride, I will quickly transport him to another scene of my exertions; for the new acquaintances he has got to make with me gradually crowd upon us, and the other persons who have not as yet taken any active part in our history also have a claim on his attention.

I will, therefore, immediately conduct him with me

THE MADMAN OF ST. JAMES'.

to London, which place I had left at the end of April to proceed to Scotland, from which I reached St. James' at the beginning of June, when I had the honour of introducing myself and my narrative to the notice of my friends for the first time.

CHAPTER VIII.

A CELEBRATED PHYSICIAN.

THE reader knows well enough the oppressive heat and noisy bustle which meet the stranger at the beginning of August when he enters the enormous capital by the City part. The confusion and the immense traffic, which is to be found nowhere else, usually astonish every foreigner, but they did not much affect me. I looked upon London now as the place in which all my hopes were centred, and which was to crown with success all the exertions which I have detailed. A larger sphere of action was opened to me by my arrival in this city, where all my present sources of interest were united, and I determined to set to work actively and quickly.

During my former stay in London I had lived with a German, a friend of mine ; now, however, in order to be master of my own time, and be perfectly independent, I went to an hotel, as near as possible to the residence of my patron, a friend of my father, the celebrated physician, Sir John ——, who was then residing in Regent Street.

158

THE MADMAN OF ST. JAMES'.

It is a comfortable feeling, on returning from a fatiguing journey, to give one's self up to repose and undisturbed meditation in a quiet and comfortable apartment; but this delightful feeling I did not experience, my mind was too unsettled and wandering, and my feelings too excited to permit peaceful thought or quiet meditation.

Before I did anything else I unburthened myself of the considerable sum of money which I had carried about me, and arranged my papers; for the following morning I wished to make my necessary visits, in order to ascertain at once how things really stood. With respect to other visits, connected with my own affairs, I did not think about them.

My first visit early the next morning was to Sir John ———; but in order to prepare him for my arrival I had forwarded my card to him the previous evening as soon as I had reached the hotel, in reply to which I received a message that my visit would give him pleasure, and that I was already expected. But in order to enlighten the reader in some degree as to the person and character of Sir John ———, I think it best to make beforehand some remarks relative to his position and sphere of action.

Sir John ———, Bart., was one of the most distinguished physicians, and also one of the most learned men, I have ever had the happiness of meeting during all my various travels. Gifted with an

THE MADMAN OF ST. JAMES'. 159

uncommonly determined character, and with a most tender heart, through indomitable industry and uninterrupted study at the best sources of medical knowledge, assisted by a clear mind, he had gained esteem and celebrity in his brilliant career. A philosopher, a physician, and a man in one person, immensely rich in rare and great experience, he was always considered a star in society, and looked up to by all of his profession.

Formerly a physician, with one of the first and most extensive connections, and also a clever and daring operator, he had only lately devoted himself with uncontrolled ardour to those unfathomable depths of study relative to mental diseases, and his endeavours to alleviate them had been crowned repeatedly with the greatest success.

He only thought and lived now to kindle afresh "the still glimmering spark," as Percy called it, which remained of the nearly-extinguished flame glowing in the minds of those who had less understanding and power of judgment than he had; and to find out and remove the causes of this malady was the task to which all his great talents were at this time devoted.

As the first physician of Bethlehem Hospital, the largest lunatic asylum in the world, fortune had favoured him; and although his duties here continually engaged him, he yet contrived to be of some general service in the world by his advice, his great kindness, and ample means. That such a man should have gained the respect and esteem of all who knew him, far and near, and realized a considerable fortune, I need not mention more particularly.

His personal appearance was as extraordinary and peculiar as his learning was extensive and his goodness remarkable. In his younger days he had been of a thoughtful and calm temper, and in his more advanced years one would have taken him at first sight to be icy cold; but this cold manner was not the effect of a chilled heart, but was produced by the daily increasing calmness and clearness of his mind. It was the pure contemplative isolation—if I may thus express myself—from external objects, and he used it to arrange his ideas without interruption, and to carry out his intentions.

Two years before he had had a fit, and could now only move about with difficulty. His hands trembled, his limbs shook slightly, and he stammered sometimes so much, that some words he could scarcely pronounce; but when he hesitated, he would pause for a moment, and quickly recover himself, and repeat his words very slowly, and apparently with much trouble. His step was uncertain; he stooped forwards; his manner of expressing himself was in general abrupt, quick, and interrupted, and was often remarkable for his extraordinary mixture of similes and short ejaculations.

THE MADMAN OF ST. JAMES'.

His greatest characteristic was his intelligent face, and the expression of his features was very often imposing and commanding; his complexion was almost ashy pale; his few remaining hairs were white as silver; his cheeks were wan and hollow, and the various bones beneath the skin could be easily traced. When he was silent, he constantly held his mouth pinched together; but when he spoke, he seemed to become quite another being, and, quick as lightning, in every line round his mouth appeared so much expression, that, with wondering astonishment, I used to gaze on this extraordinary play of the muscles. But the most remarkable peculiarity of his whole appearance was the eye. His eyes, greyish-blue, round, and rather large, appeared, at first sight, and when he looked down, dull, almost dim, nearly faded; as soon, however, as he fixed an attentive glance on any body in earnest conversation, or while he examined a patient, particularly with regard to the state of his mind, one became almost dazzled by the peculiar brilliancy of his steadfast look, which was like the sharp glance of an eagle, and seemed to search and pierce through one. Thus he obtained great power over others, especially over those patients who were subjected to these inquiring looks. When once that look was calmly and steadily fixed on any one, it pierced irresistibly every barrier of the mind; and thus he read every thought and feeling in the heart of his patient. This single look, which betrayed

VOL. II.

his clear mind and powerful intelligence, was sufficient to ensure his purpose being carried out at once; and no one—not even the roughest and most intractable —was able to withstand it: he acquired power over everybody.

But severe as he was as a physician, determined in his purposes, and unyielding in their execution, he was, as a friend, sincere; as a man, most kind; forbearing towards the errors of others, and, above all things, never inordinately vain and conceited; never malevolent or morose, like many of his profession; never bearing malice; always frank, always candid, always cheerful, and so far an amiable man, and one worthy to be imitated.

He had, however, acquired one peculiarity in his later years—my father, at least, had never remarked it —he loved a joke, this serious man; he liked nothing so well in society as a good joke, to which he himself was much prone; never, however, overstepping the bounds of truth and propriety. Whoever saw him for the first time, and heard him talk, could never, by any possibility, have imagined him to be that great, celebrated deep-thinker he was known to be. Such was the style of his usual conversation; although always intellectual, and permitting persons to guess more than they heard, it was not studied or forced —it was just what came uppermost in his mind.

This original and genial man was loved and respected by those who knew him; wondered at by

THE MADMAN OF ST. JAMES'.   163

those who did *not* know him; feared by his patients, but followed by their blessings; for they knew that he performed what he promised, and that the remembrance of their sufferings was not lost in his heart.

At the hour when I knew him to be at home, I went to his house, and his valet having told me his master had already inquired twice for me, I entered his room without being announced—a privilege which was accorded to but very few. I found him in his consulting-room, sitting in an arm-chair, and ready dressed for driving out, as usual. The walls were covered with exquisite paintings, and the whole house, in its furniture and appointments, bore witness to the best taste.

Hearing the door closed by which I had entered, he half turned round towards me, and holding his head a little bent forward, as he usually did, he held out his trembling right hand to me, and said, in his accustomed kind and good-natured voice,—

"Ah! here, at last, is little Job!" for so he always called me, although I am neither little, nor is my name Job; but Job had been, in former years, the nickname of my father, and from him had been transmitted to me; for with Sir John ——, as is generally the case with great men, the remembrances of his youth were sacred, and, therefore, I could but feel it to be an honour when the old gentleman allowed himself this little joke at my expense. "Ah! here, at last, is little Job!" he exclaimed, "with his

M 2

164 THE MADMAN OF ST. JAMES'.

mysteries of St. James', eh? It is extraordinary that everybody in the world has secrets, and I never had one in my life."

"But you have known plenty belonging to other people instead," I replied, shaking him heartily by the hand.

"He who hides much from other people, hides generally the most from himself. And now, little Job, how are you?"

"Thank you, heartily, sir. When I am with you I am always well."

"And once more safe here again? Ever travelling: funny fancy. Always most contented and comfortable at home. Glad to see you. How are they up there?"

By this he meant St. James', because it lay to the north of London.

I delivered the messages to him with which I had been entrusted, as well as the letter already mentioned of Mr. Lorenz, which he laid aside; and I was just going to refer to the strange events which had brought me to his side, when he said, smiling,—

"Plenty of time for that, little Job. How is Mr. Derby, the under-physician? Does he still continue to classify humanity into eighths? and does he still wear his little blue c—coat?"

"Yes, he has still his eighths, and wears a blue coat."

"Bad word for me that: c—coat. I can, I can

hardly get it out, Job. Hem! The blue c—coat! Do you know the story of the blue c—coat, eh?"

"No," I answered smiling, for I knew the story would now certainly come.

"What! you have been in St. James' and don't know that? Well, you shall hear it now, then. Formerly, when I was up there—well, rather long ago—the following occurrence took place:—Mr. Derby always wore a blue c—coat, for he only had a black one besides, and that only made its appearance on grand occasions—it was the Sunday one. Hem! It was soon a settled thing that Mr. Derby should go by the name of " the blue c—coat." On one holiday his beloved patients determined to play him a trick with his blue coat. One of them, a merry fellow, who, besides being mad, had the reputation of being a wit, wrote a comedy, and called it "The Blue Coat." To perform in such comedies is always a favourite amusement with crazy folks—hem !— and especially those at St. James'. Hem! You smile, little Job. I used to play comedy too ; was the lover —always played the lover. Ha, ha! The parts were distributed and studied. The skittle-ground was the theatre, the audience seated, actors ready, but the chief thing was wanting—the most necessary part of the wardrobe, the blue c— coat! Yes, now what was to be done? 'Be quiet,' said the wit; 'Mr. Derby is asleep, it is just the time he takes his afternoon nap; I will try and get it out of his room.' All right. Steals into his room. Ha! there is the coat on the chair; just the thing! Takes it like a juggler. Runs back in triumph to the skittle-ground. 'Here it is gentlemen—the blue c—coat!' Ha, ha! Is received with applause; clapping of hands too; otherwise it is nothing. But now is the point of the story. Mr. Derby wakes, wants to go out, and to pay his visits; but where is the c—coat? Mr. Derby looks about, but he can't find it. Mr. Derby gets angry; he cannot understand any joke being played on his person, and shouts, and raves, and makes a noise, and rings the whole house together. Just then Mr. Elliotson and Mr. Lorenz happen to pass by, and now a general search begins. But the old boys suspect the trick, and laugh already beforehand. 'Gentlemen,' says Mr. Derby, 'this is no laughing matter; it is despicable, gentlemen. It is a stupid joke, gentlemen. I can't go my rounds in my shirt sleeves; and you laugh at it, gentlemen!' Enough. The c—coat can't be found, and Mr. Derby is obliged, in his rage, to put on the black one. Ha, ha, ha! a black coat and nankeen trousers!—ha, ha! But Mr. Derby is cunning; he fancies there is a trick, does not know who has played it, and rushes out, we all after him. Now into the park. Ha, ha! 'Gentlemen, what is going on in the skittle-ground?' And then it is all out. He finds them just at the c—c—catastrophe. Ha, ha! 'My blue c—coat!' cries Mr. Derby, in an awful voice, 'my blue c—coat play

THE MADMAN OF ST. JAMES'. 167

comedy? Gentlemen, see here, you are witnesses to this infamous outrage against my blue c—coat. Go immediately, Mr. Wit, and take it back to its proper place. Mr. Jones, five pailfuls—you understand me.' And the wit went and carried the coat back, and received his five pails of cold water with the air of a m—martyr. Ha, ha, ha! Now, little Job, you know the story of Mr. Derby's blue c—coat."

"Yes, Sir John, I do indeed, and shall not forget it easily. Ha, ha!"

And we both laughed immoderately over the history of the blue coat; it would have been impossible to have refrained from laughing at the sight of the wonderful and inimitable gestures of the relator.

After the old gentleman had thus unburdened himself, he said seriously,—

"Now we have laughed—laughing is very good for the health, I know that well—and now for business."

"Yes, sir, I indeed owe it to you to explain the reason of my conduct, in writing to you and requesting you ——"

"Stop, little Job—stop! Has the story anything to do with me? Does it concern me at all? Know so many old stories already, have not the least desire to hear any new ones."

"No, sir, no; it is true, you have nothing to do with it."

"Well, then, I don't want to know it. Everybody has his reasons for doing anything out of the way. You, too ——"

168 THE MADMAN OF ST. JAMES'.

"But it is a most important affair, sir."

"Certainly; I am sure it is! If I can be of any use to you, or serve you in any way, I am ready—it has got time until then; it won't eat my little Job up—ha, ha! But now I have got something for you too, and that is most important for us both; you just come at the right time. Look now," said he, taking a letter from his desk, and unfolding it; "I received this letter yesterday from one of my old patients, the Marquis of Seymour."

"Heavens!" cried I, starting back involuntarily. The old baronet looked at me in his peculiar, searching way.

"Well, do you know?—do you already know what I want?"

"No, sir. Until now I have only heard of him ——"

"Bravo! Just it; always find the right man on the right spot. Are you sufficiently recovered from your astonishment to listen to me quietly?"

"Yes, sir," said I, trying to compose myself; for by his look continually fixed on me, I saw that I must have betrayed much uneasiness.

"Well, you see, his son tells me in this letter— they say he is the heir—hem!—this Lord Mortimer —that his father has come to London, and gone to his country house some few miles from town. Now, do you know what for?"

"I can guess, sir."

THE MADMAN OF ST. JAMES'.   ·   169

"Well, then, to be cured by me—Ha, ha, ha! Every one wants to be cured, as if that was such an easy matter. 'Here am I, Mr. Doctor; now come and let the case go as quick as possible; here are my thanks'—Ha, ha! As if I, poor old cripple as I am, could go there every day, when I have got so much to do already here, that I should like to have eight feet and four heads. But still this Lord Mortimer is rather reasonable; he tells me his father is suffering from irritation of the nerves; every noise frightens him—every strange face makes him uneasy—hem! Naturally, *that*, of course, must be irritation of the nerves! Poor nerves! Every one thinks he knows best about his own illness, and there is no occasion to believe a doctor—pretty business! But I say this Lord Mortimer is a little reasonable, for he is of the opinion— in which I perfectly agree with him—that if I could not attend his father myself, I might send a serious gentleman of my school instead—as if I were a schoolmaster! But the word 'school' explains it sufficiently"—and he made a characteristic movement by touching his forehead with his forefinger. "And I was to request him to remain with his father for some days, for the sake of making the necessary observations."

"Well, sir?" I asked, as he still looked at me searchingly, without doubt to try and read from my countenance how I liked his proposal.

"Well, little Job, I have chosen *you* as this serious

THE MADMAN OF ST. JAMES'.

gentleman; you have just the look and the manner that does for such—such—such weak nerves! What do you say to my proposal of taking my recommendation with you on your journey, and taking a little drive out there this morning? You will find there a very good table."

"But allow me, sir," said I quickly, "I *must* confide to you my secret."

"No, no, little Job, you must *not;* I don't want to know it yet. For once you must act alone, and when you have exhausted your own wisdom, I will write my opinion, if you are a clever man or not—eh?"

"Well, well, sir; I will act ——"

"Yes, sir, you shall;—now, still a few more words about this man. Known him a long time; proud aris—aris—aristocrat, bad husband; partial father, but rich—very rich; may be made a duke, and the world says *amen!* But I don't; have always had my own suspicions—hem!"

"What suspicions, sir?"

"What suspicions? Yes, you shall tell me that when we see each other again. It is not all quite right in his family; something about it was once in the papers."

"Ah! I know, sir; I know."

"You know, little Job? That is a mistake; four years ago you were not yet here."

"But nevertheless I know it, sir. As true as I live, I know it."

THE MADMAN OF ST. JAMES'. 171

"Well, then, all the better for you; we will talk again about the matter. Will you visit him now, Mr. Doctor?"

"Certainly," I exclaimed; "immediately."

"Ha, ha! that is right—that is as it should be. Yes, go," he resumed, with a sudden seriousness, which was almost severe. "Probe him, sound him deeper and deeper, with a sure hand—you understand me. If *you* cannot fathom him, remember *I am here too.* In a few days I shall expect to hear from you. Have you lunched yet?"

"Yes, sir; yes."

"But not with me." And the old man rang a small silver bell which stood before him on the table, and ordered luncheon to be brought up for me; for he always took his meals by himself, breakfasting at seven o'clock in the morning, and dining at precisely seven o'clock in the evening, that, as he said, he might not lose too much time.

I had, however, no wish to eat or to drink; I should have preferred to drive off immediately, but I could not refuse, and I remained. During luncheon the name of Sir William Graham occurred to me.

"My dear sir," I said, "do you happen to know a Sir William Graham, formerly a celebrated solicitor or barrister in London?"

"I did know him, little Job—hem!—are the oysters good, eh? I did know him—why do you look at me so?—two months ago only—was an excellent man—my friend—my solicitor—but now—

172   THE MADMAN OF ST. JAMES'.

an apoplectic fit—just such a one as I had, but not so fortunate as I—one more—then another—nobody could help him—dead!"

"What?" I cried, rising from my chair in speechless astonishment.

"Yes, little Job. Could *you* help it? *I* could not—who could? It was God's will."

And the good old man looked at me with such a truly sorrowful but resigned look, that I could not help going up to him, and grasping his hand.

"And has he left no children?" I asked.

"No, little Job, no children; a brother inherits baronetcy and all."

"And who is this brother?"

"Formerly a clergyman, it is said; I have never seen him; when I visited Sir William he was on a journey; is said to be a good man—the property this time will fall into good hands—glad of it."

"And where did Sir William Graham live?"

"After he had retired from his profession, and that is a long time ago,—he only managed my affairs and those of a few of his old friends, out of kindness and pure custom,—he had a country seat six or eight miles from Seymour Castle, where you are going; you will be able to hear all about him there, if you want to know anything more particular concerning him. And now, little Job, have you had enough?"

"Quite, sir."

THE MADMAN OF ST. JAMES'. 173

"Well, now we must go to our work; I to Bethlehem, and you to Jerusalem." And the old man laughed heartily at this most extraordinary notion.

"Good morning, sir; I shall see you, then, again in a few days, and then my secret ——"

"There is no hurry for that. Good morning, little Job; my carriage will take you there in an hour's time. But listen: don't run so fast, you will break your neck—in an hour—do you hear?—goodbye!"

I ran down stairs as fast as I could run, and arrived in my own room at the hotel almost breathless. Was my being sent to the marquis accident, or was it sent from above? I do not know. One feeling alone possessed me, the feeling of inward satisfaction at the realization of a part of my most ardent wishes, of gratitude to Providence, and a firm determination of going further in the path I had begun thus to tread with seriousness and care.

With Bob I quickly made the necessary arrangements, put my toilette and my luggage into proper order, and in an hour's time I was sitting in Sir John's carriage on the road to Seymour Castle, the country seat of the rich and powerful Marquis of Seymour.

CHAPTER IX.

A DISTINGUISHED PATIENT AND A KIND SON.

" Sound him, deeper and deeper, and if you cannot fathom him, remember I am here too."

This very remarkable expression of Sir John ——, who most likely knew something of the state of mind of his old patient, continually occurred to me during my drive to Seymour Castle. I could not get rid of the thoughts it occasioned.

" I will sound him," I said to myself; "sound the very depths of his heart and the secret recesses of his dark soul; and as I know beforehand the unfathomed depths of his most secret thoughts, I shall soon manage to bring them all to light. Sir John has only, in his case, suspicion; I have a certainty to work upon. For this experienced man, this master of the human heart, this suspicion may be sufficient, and he may soon discover all that remains concealed; I, however, possess the power to unlock his inmost heart, and this I will use to pierce to the deepest recesses, and I will abide there until I can cast all from it that may stand in the way of the good deed

I have undertaken to perform. But first, before I touch the wound with my probe and begin my operations, I must gain his confidence; without that all would be in vain, and, like a slippery eel, he would escape my grasp. If this succeeds, and he sees that I go to work with zeal and a desire to help him, even then he may not trust me; *then* it will be time for me to break the seal of the past; then my conduct must be cautious and firm, kind and forbearing.

"And if this does not succeed, and I find him— which I trust may not be the case—a hardened sinner, acting wrong with cold premeditation, then I will break by force the icy covering of his heart, and it will not be my fault if, instead of his cons ler and friend, I become his evil genius. For I shall not only have to alleviate the disease which consumes him, but I shall have also to destroy the effects of the poison which has gone out from him, and made the lives of so many others miserable and unhappy.

"Courage, Percy! Courage, Ellinor! Courage, Graham! I am now your advocate, sent by God to plead your cause. Your hour and my hour is come, and may God grant that I may be able to act mercifully."

And while I was thus occupied with my plans and with thoughts of my mode of conduct, the carriage rolled on quickly over the gravel, and stopped before the grand entrance of the country-seat of the

Marquis of Seymour before I had come to the end of half my cogitations.

I had been leaning back in the carriage while thus reflecting, and even before I had time to look around me, several servants, among whom was the steward, hastened immediately to the carriage door, and helped me to alight, for they had most likely recognized Sir John's carriage.

I was now in front of the magnificent building of Seymour Castle; it was old, but still in excellent preservation, and commanded an extensive view over a smiling, green, far-spreading country, while behind it was a thickly-planted, dismal, and solitary wood.

"You come from Sir John —— ?" began the steward, with a bow, " do you not, sir? Oh, sir! we have been anxiously expecting your arrival."

" As Sir John —— himself is not well, I have come in his stead," I replied; "but who has been anxiously expecting me?"

" The marquis, sir, Lord Mortimer, and, indeed, all of us: it is high time some one came," added he, in a whisper. "Will you allow me to have your luggage taken to your room? It is to be hoped you are going to remain, sir?"

" I intend to do so for a time;" I answered, and ascended the stone steps to the hall; while one of the servants immediately went on before me to take my valise up stairs, and at my bidding Sir John's carriage returned to London.

We entered the house; every passage, staircase, and floor was covered with thick green baize, so that not a step might be heard. Every door shut and opened noiselessly; no one could be heard speaking; an unbroken, uncomfortable silence reigned throughout the whole house, as if it were either a grave or the place of repose of some tyrant who had retired to rest, before whom every sign of life must vanish, and every sound must be hushed.

The steward conducted me in silence to an apartment on the first floor, the windows of which, however, looked out on nothing better than the dismal dark wood. As soon as my conductor had entered the room with me, he shut the door cautiously, as well as the windows which were wide open, and then placed a chair for me.

"I am extremely sorry," he began, "that Lord Mortimer should just now not happen to be at home; he wished so much to speak to the physician who was expected, before he should see his lordship the Marquis."

"And where is Lord Mortimer?"

"He is out hunting, sir, with a few friends from the neighbourhood;" said the man, with a very sorrowful expression of face, and looking thoughtfully out of the window into the dismal wood beyond.

"Oh! indeed! hunting! Lord Mortimer hunts a good deal, I suppose?"

"Well, sir, we have been here only a few days;

but it is his favourite amusement; and perhaps he wants some sort of recreation sometimes, for my lord frightens him as well as the rest of us."

These words the old man appeared to utter with some hesitation.

"He frightens him?" I repeated; "Well, but how? I should think if his lordship were so seriously ill, it would make Lord Mortimer more anxious than frightened."

"No, sir; but yes, perhaps so, sir! But that is his lordship's extraordinary malady, that he puts all who are around him in a state of the greatest fear and agitation. He himself gets no rest by night or by day, and so we cannot have any either; and, because he is afraid of the least noise, and in a state of continual alarm, we must all, of course, be as quiet as possible."

"What is he afraid of then?"

"Yes, sir! that is just what I do not know. Every night we take it in turns to watch by him, and he whose turn it is must either sleep when he sleeps, or keep awake and be merry just as his lordship is in the humour to sleep or to be merry himself. You should just hear how he asks every minute if one is still there, and awake, and if he has not seen or heard anything. At first, Lord Mortimer would not leave him; but he could not bear to be with him for any length of time, as my lord believes he is constantly seeing or hearing something in his room which completely unnerves him."

"Well, what does he see or hear then? do speak plainly!"

"Well, then, ghosts, I think. It is a dreadful state to be in, sir! You should just be present."

"I believe it. And how long is it since all this began?"

"Oh, as to when it really first began, I don't quite know, sir; but it is some time since—I should think more than a year."

"And how did it begin?"

"Quite gradually; one hardly remarked it at the time, sir. At first his lordship began to change continually his place of residence, then his room, his attendants, his bed; he was never quiet, and never contented with anything. Then he began to get nervous, and particularly to be afraid of death; and then of strangers, and would not see anybody, until it came at last to the state in which he now is."

The old man had become quite pale while telling me all this.

"And was Lord Mortimer always with him?" I inquired.

"Yes, sir, and—between ourselves, sir, one night when his lordship was very nervous he told me that —he was more afraid of Lord Mortimer than anybody or anything else."

"Indeed! And do you not know the reason for all this?"

The man shrugged his shoulders, and said with some hesitation and stammering,—

"No, sir, no! At least—no particular reason. But that is just what, I believe, Lord Mortimer wished to speak to you about before you saw my lord."

"And when will Lord Mortimer return?" I asked.

"At three or four o'clock, sir, I believe."

"And now it is half-past one o'clock, therefore, he will not be in for two or three hours. That is too long to wait; I should like to see his lordship now—and besides, I can speak with Lord Mortimer afterwards."

"That is true. But please, sir, when Lord Mortimer comes back, will you tell him that it was your own positive wish to go to the marquis ——"

"Depend upon it; I will be sure to tell him so."

"Well then, sir, I will inquire directly if the marquis can receive you."

The man went out, and I was left a few minutes alone.

"The wind blows from a different quarter to what I expected," thought I; "it is not a bad wind for me; I shall have to tack about a good deal, but it will be easier than I thought. My work has already been begun for me, I see—all right!"

THE MADMAN OF ST. JAMES'.   181

The steward returned, and announced that the marquis was willing to receive my visit immediately.

We ascended a staircase, for the room of the patient was just above mine, and had just the same miserable prospect over the dismal, solitary wood. Although my arrival had been announced to him, and the steward opened the door as softly as possible, still I could hear, while standing in the corridor, the broken words of a perfectly toneless, cold, almost expiring voice proceeding from the chamber.

"Be quiet," it said,—"who is that? Ha! is it you, Paul? Do open the door gently—you frighten me."

I entered softly; but at first I could hardly see anything; for the room, gloomy enough of itself, was so darkened by the long, heavy, green silk curtains, drawn closely before the windows, that scarcely a ray of light could pierce through them. The entire floor of the room was covered with a moss-like velvet carpet, also of green; and, although it was the month of August, still in the grate glowed a large fire. The chimney-piece was of black marble, and a large mirror was placed over it. I also perceived in the room a nasty disagreeable smell,—which even the abundance of perfumes used could not subdue,—produced by the condensed air, which was never renewed, for the Marquis would never allow a single window to be opened.

182   THE MADMAN OF ST. JAMES.'

"The doctor from London, my lord," said the steward, making a low bow. "You ordered ——"

"That is enough, Paul; enough, William. You may go away—I will have you called when—but softly—do go out softly—softly—you frighten me!"

I looked in the direction from whence this frosty voice came. I was seeking for the man who was afraid. Close by the fire, in an arm-chair, lay a form enveloped in fur from head to foot; the face alone I gradually began to distinguish; I strained my eyes to try and find something in the features resembling those I loved—but it was impossible: this face was hardly like that of a living human being, it resembled far more the face of the dead.

It was deadly pale, of an ashy hue, long, and covered with many and deep wrinkles; only a few hairs, and those silvery white, remained on his head; his forehead was extremely large, but produced a particularly disagreeable impression; for it was disproportioned, too broad, too high, and too prominent.

His timid-looking eyes, although not small, were almost hidden in their deep sockets by the bushy eyebrows which overshadowed them.

"Ah, sir!" said the patient, in a more animated voice, "you come from my friend, Sir John ——?"

"Yes, my lord! I bring your lordship the respectful compliments of one who is also my friend;

THE MADMAN OF ST. JAMES'. 183

his numerous engagements and his own state of health prevent him from having the pleasure himself of——"

"Enough, enough; I am quite contented. Take a seat, sir."

I looked round for a chair, but, from the darkness of the room, could not find one; therefore, I still remained for a few moments standing before him.

"Sit down, sir," exclaimed he, in a loud, and, as it appeared to me, too commanding a tone.

"Not yet, my lord," I answered; "a physician must have all his senses about him when he is with his patient; allow me first to draw back the curtains a little."

And, while speaking, I stepped quickly to the window, and, without further ceremony, by means of a cord which was hanging there, drew aside the one half of the curtains, which flew back with a shrill noise. Immediately a bright, but certainly not a dazzling gleam of light penetrated the spacious apartment; for behind the green curtains I found there were also white ones drawn closely across the windows.

"Stop," said the marquis, frightened in the highest degree; "what are you doing? And what a noise!"

"It is necessary and unavoidable, my lord——"

"Close them again, close them quickly, I say. Light? Ha, ha! I cannot bear the light."

184   THE MADMAN OF ST. JAMES'.

"No, my lord, I shall *not* close them, and you *must* bear it."

And I placed myself before him, so that the light so hastily admitted might not dazzle him. And I now quietly looked at him; but I was almost frightened at the timid, startled, restless look which met mine. His eyes seemed to be in constant motion; they wandered nervously round the apartment, and at last remained fixed upon me with a troubled and anxious expression. I could not trace in him the least resemblance to Percy's noble and handsome face; but I could not observe him longer, for he immediately began,—

"You take a good deal upon yourself, sir. I am not accustomed to have my orders disobeyed. I cannot bear the light."

These words, spoken evidently from obstinacy, made me feel some confidence in the line of conduct I had adopted. I looked at him calmly, but firmly, and answered,—

"I cannot judge of your state and observe you without light."

"Observe me? Ha!"

"Yes, my lord, observe you. You have wished to see a physician that he may do you some good; but a doctor will not be ruled; he acts as he thinks right himself. You must have light; and in that, as well as every other point, your will must submit to mine

THE MADMAN OF ST. JAMES'. 185

—that is to say, as long as I am your doctor, and you are my patient."

He looked at me now in the greatest surprise, but without saying a word, for he seemed to be more astonished than angry.

"I was glad at first," he remarked, "that Sir John did not come himself; he has got a withering look, such a determined will, and such a domineering tone! But you—*you* ——"

I did not allow him to finish his sentence, but said,—

"Not withering; it only appears so, my lord. It is, in fact, only reflective and searching, and such looks a physician must have when he wishes to penetrate the hidden depths of the—the ——"

"What, sir—eh?"

I would not let this disturb me, but quietly continued :—

"When he wishes to penetrate the hidden depths and sources of human suffering. Must not his look be keen, when he seeks and chooses the best and most suitable remedy for the patient before him? and the keener my look is, the more advantage you will derive from it."

"Sit down, sir; it is enough. I see it does not do to contend with you. But wait, first; please will you stir the fire a little, it is so cold here."

I took up the bright poker and stirred the fire,

186   THE MADMAN OF ST. JAMES'.

although the room was already so hot that drops of
perspiration trickled from my forehead; I then took
a chair, and seated myself just before him.

"And now, my lord," said I, " allow me to request
you to tell me every particular of your state."

"Tell you? You speak strangely—very strangely;
never did anybody expect that from me. I should
think that you might just as well question me;—
question me about it, and I shall answer what I
think proper."

"No, my lord, that will not do. That is my opinion. My questions will come afterwards. You must
speak first."

"But, heavens! what am I to tell you, then?"

He drew a deep breath, and moved about uneasily
and impatiently in his chair. I knew very well he
had no positive cause of complaint, but a mind bur-
dened with its own guilt does not like to give itself
out in words; it throws all its pains upon some imaginary or pretended illness of the body, and never
dares to say frankly what it suffers.

"Well," continued he, " if you will have it so;—
but I should think you might now close those curtains
again."

"No, my lord; I must insist on it. I beg you to
begin—boldly, sincerely, faithfully; we are alone."

He appeared now to be making a violent effort;
and with difficulty brought out at last a whole series
of indistinct complaints, of which I considered only

one to have some foundation, and that was, want of air, and a feeling as if a heavy weight lay upon his breast.

I now began to ask him some questions, to which I received but very short answers. I then requested him to give me his hand; he gave it me in silence, looked at me inquiringly during my examination, and shuddered perceptibly when I touched him.

Notwithstanding the fur and the heat of the room, his hand was cold and clammy; the pulse was strong, extremely full and slow, just as it usually is in the case of any one who is going to have an apoplectic fit. I leaned back in my chair, and reflected for some minutes. "You must endeavour to win his confidence by giving him some sort of alleviation," thought I.

"How do you find me, sir?" he asked, hesitatingly.

"I do not find you seriously ill, my lord," was my reply; "but, allow me to ask you a few questions. You sleep but little?"

"Hardly at all."

"But you never take any exercise?"

"Well, no."

"When you wish to go to sleep, some indistinct vision always hovers before your eyes?"

"Indistinct? well, yes, sir—yes; go on—go on."

"Your thoughts dwell too much on certain subjects?"

188   THE MADMAN OF ST. JAMES'.

"Well, what subjects?"

"On your sufferings."

"Well, yes, sir."

"And neither in word, nor deed, nor thought, can you find any consolation. Is it not so?"

"Sir! what are you saying? You understand my state perfectly. Yes, it is so."

"And why do you not tell me this yourself?"

"Ha! how could I tell out everything like that? I did not know you. But now, already I feel I begin to know you. Ah! it is difficult to speak like that. But how do you know all this? Who told you it was so?"

"Nobody told me; I have read it."

"Read it, sir?" And, with a look of pain and horror, as if an adder had stung him, he half rose from his chair. "Read it? Where? Where?"

"Calm yourself, my lord; I have only read it on your face."

"What? on my face? Does my face speak so intelligibly?"

"For me it is like a book."

"Ha! that is not true, sir! Give me that—there—a looking-glass; it is yonder, there—on the table."

I took hold of the round hand glass and held it before him. He started back and covered his face with both his hands.

"Is that my face?" he murmured, in a half-choked voice.

THE MADMAN OF ST. JAMES'. 189

I looked at him quietly, and I must say my look was full of pity.

"Speak, sir! only speak—only speak! Your silence is more dreadful than your words. Who are you? What do you want of me? You can read well."

I looked at him more earnestly; our looks met; he wished to avoid mine, but he could not; an invincible power—perhaps that of his awakening soul —seemed to enchain him. I really, now, could read in his face—there was something intelligible there for me—and he also appeared to understand mine. I had succeeded in drawing him out of himself, and had penetrated the veil of his hidden soul.

"Listen," he continued; "I will now tell you something; but, come nearer—nearer still—quite close."

And he whispered in my ear, which I bent near him, in so low a tone, that I could with difficulty understand his words.

"What I wanted to tell you—yes—speak softly— do not tell anybody about what we have been speaking of—least of all, to my son Mortimer when he comes back. We two, quite alone, will keep it secret. Listen! We two, quite alone—ah! I have still much to tell you. I am an unhappy old man— have you already read that also?"

"My lord!" I answered, really touched by the painful expression of anxiety depicted on his shrunken features, and, grasping his thin hand, which I pressed warmly—perhaps too warmly. "You are right, my lord; we will confide in each other; nobody need have anything at all to do with our concerns, except you—the patient, and me—the doctor."

He leaned back, and I heard a deep-drawn sigh.

"Ah!" said he, "I believe you are able to help me, but everything is against me."

I again reflected for some moments.

"My lord," I resumed, "I have now got some arrangements to make for to-day; to-morrow we will speak together further."

"To-morrow? Why not to-day?—why not immediately?"

"No; it will not do. First, I must procure for you that which will give you relief and rest; then we will go on with our conversation, which then we can continue more easily."

"But you will come to me this evening? Ah! the evening and—the night—ah!"

He shivered, as if an icy chill affected him; his lips trembled, and his whole face became even a degree paler than it was before.

"Do not be afraid any more, my lord," was my reply; "I shall always be near you; and, besides, you can have me called to you at any moment. Bear your misfortunes like a man; with God's help we will overcome all that distresses you."

"With God's help! Yes; oh, yes!—and *all?*—

THE MADMAN OF ST. JAMES'. 191

Ah! that is very much! But it is well—it is very well, sir. And what have you got to prescribe for me?"

" Light—air; and you must also take exercise, and I shall take from you a few ounces of blood."

" Blood—blood! why blood? I did not think my illness lay in my blood."

" Neither does it. No."

" But where then?"

" I will tell you that later, my lord; for the first thing I must do is to make your half-frozen blood circulate more freely; you must breathe fresh air, and let the light of day shine on you."

" That cannot be, sir; the light hates me."

" It *must be,* my lord; the light does *not* hate you; —you, on the contrary, hate the light. In a word, I will have it so: *I* require it, and *you* require it."

" You speak very positively, Mr. Doctor."

" It is my duty, my lord. Have you any objection to take a drive?"

" A drive? what, with horses? In the name of Heaven, no! Where do you wish to drive me to?"

" Ha, ha!" thought I, but I pretended not to notice his alarm, and immediately added,—

" Well, we might get a wheel-chair from London, and one of your servants, my lord, might wheel it up and down the garden. In the mean time we will have the room well aired, or, rather, you had better move to another apartment in the front of the house, which looks over the park. These thick green curtains must be taken away, and white muslin must be put up. Yes; so it must be."

"White curtains?—air?—another room? You seem to be very strange."

I went to the door and opened it.

"Where are you going? Stop!" he cried.

"I only want to call your servants," I replied. And I called in the steward, who was standing without, and repeated to him my orders for all I wished to have done, and then began to make preparations for bleeding my patient. Contrary to my expectations, he submitted quietly to all I wished to do. In a few minutes I had finished; he was placed again in his arm-chair, and carried by his servants into the garden; and once again the bright sunshine fell upon his venerable head. A messenger was then sent to London to procure a convenient wheel-chair, and immediate arrangements were made for his occupying a more pleasant apartment on the sunny side of the building.

It was on the same day, towards four o'clock in the afternoon. I had already dined; at my request my dinner had been served in my own room; and I had just come to that part of the park which lay at the side of the castle, when, sitting beneath an acacia tree on one of the garden seats, I heard loud voices announcing the noisy return of the hunting party.

THE MADMAN OF ST. JAMES'. 193

The servants immediately hurried out to receive the snorting horses and yelping dogs, when I heard a loud and rather disagreeable voice call for the steward. Immediately I instinctively felt that this was the voice of Lord Mortimer, Percy's brother. The thought made me tremble; but I had not time to think of my own feelings; for, on account of the speaker's near approach, I was obliged to be an unseen hearer of a conversation which immediately followed, and which possessed for me at this moment the greatest interest.

In a tone which was intended to be familiar, the voice said to the steward, who had quickly hurried up,—

"Anything new, old fellow? Anything new taken place there up yonder?"

"Yes, Lord Mortimer; the doctor from London is arrived."

"Ho, ho! where is he? Did you tell him I wished to speak with him first—before he—you know?"

"Oh, yes, sir! but you were so long absent, and my lord wanted him so much—that——"

"What?" But surely he has not yet been to him —eh?"

"I could not help it, my lord."

"By Jove, is this the way you obey my orders?" And then I heard distinctly the switching of a riding whip, as it whistled over the grey head of the old servant.

VOL. II.   o

194
THE MADMAN OF ST. JAMES'.

"Oh, please! don't, my lord—I entreat—I beg of you—I could not help it."

"Hold your tongue, you glutton! All you rascals cram yourselves from the rising to the setting of the sun. But wait! When the sun rises you will have work enough. But what did he say to him? Of course, you stopped in the room?"

"Not a moment, my lord; I know nothing at all about it."

"You cursed wretch!—what took place? What did he say?"

"I really don't know, sir, what he said; but he bled the marquis, and gave some orders about the other room being arranged. His lordship is sitting yonder in the garden."

"Sitting in the garden?—another room? Are you mad? How is that possible?"

"I am astonished enough myself, but it is just as I say."

"Ha! curse it! unlucky that I was not at home! Where is the fellow? Is it the old one himself?"

"No, my lord, but a friend of his."

"Young or old?"

"About thirty, I should think. But very decided, my lord—very decided!"

"Very decided! very decided!" mimicked the voice; "and you are very stupid! very stupid! Where is he now?"

"Without doubt in his own room."

THE MADMAN OF ST. JAMES'.   195

"Without doubt you are a blockhead. Hem!
get away—all right, we will have another talk yet
together; let the bell ring for dinner."

"The bell, sir? But his lordship ——"

"Let the bell ring, I say—directly, or—I have
three visitors—quick!"

Here ended this very edifying conversation. The
bell began to sound; but it seemed to me not quite
so loud as dinner-bells usually are. Then again all
was quiet.

This was a slight specimen of Lord Mortimer's
manners. "Well, little Job," thought I, "you also
will have the honour of seeing soon his lordship's
most excellent son—the rising sun—face to face!"
And with this I went to my own room, where I
remained for about two hours, writing up my journal,
when the door suddenly opened, and, without being
announced, the tall form of Lord Mortimer entered
the room.

I was struck at first with his appearance, for Mortimer resembled his brother Percy very much; but
it was only a likeness as to form, for otherwise he did
not resemble him in the least. He was tall, and
powerfully made; his forehead and mouth were like
Percy's forehead and mouth, but how entirely different
was the expression of his face from that of his brother,
whom I knew so well, and had learned to love so
dearly! In Percy's face every line and every feature
bore the evidence of a noble mind, of great inward

o 2

196 THE MADMAN OF ST. JAMES'.

feeling; his warmth of heart beamed forth in his open, handsome features; at first sight one saw the high aspirations of his freeborn, soaring mind and the depths of his tender heart: but here was no expression of thought or feeling, nor any impress of what was peaceful, agreeable, or intellectual. A wild, untamed, passionate expression was on that face; the moral and intellectual, the pure and ennobling expression had left no trace there, perhaps had never been called forth. His hair hung in disorder round his well-shaped head; his forehead, more shameless than courageous, was wanting in that attractive and fascinating grace which a thoughtful, high forehead usually possesses. His grey eyes looked sharply round, as if they insisted on unquestioning obedience; and round his mouth and the lips, which were strangely pressed together, lay something so haughty and contemptuous, that one immediately understood the point on which his proud heart turned: he considered the world as the slave of every change of his humour.

Besides this, Lord Mortimer had but just left the dinner table;—he had been drinking; his cheeks glowed, and his words came thick. He was even less a human being than usual, and inspired me at once with a feeling of disgust I could with difficulty repress.

His costume consisted of the usual English scarlet hunting-coat, buttoned up to the chin, white leather breeches, and topboots with large spurs; his cap was on his head, and he kept it there.

"Good day, sir," said he, throwing himself into an arm-chair. "I must praise your attention in coming here so quickly."

"Rather praise Sir John ——, for he alone hurried my visit by lending me his carriage."

"Ah! very good of him—but I hear you have been already with the marquis—I am sorry—I left strict orders—however, I can still tell you enough. How do you find him? hopeless—is not that your opinion?"

"Decidedly not, sir," I answered firmly and seriously; "on the contrary, I indulge some hope ——"

"Ha! that he may become—perfectly mad, you mean?"

I regarded the speaker with a quiet look, but with an expressive one also, I think, and kept my eyes fixed on his haughty face; but Lord Mortimer bore it all without shrinking. It was stone I was gazing on. That heart was only open to poisoned arrows. He even looked at me fixedly himself, and without the least embarrassment.

"Let it be, doctor," he resumed; "you wish to tranquillize—to console me—that is kind of you; but you need not use your usual craft with me. Always tell me the truth, and remember, a ruin mouldering as this is must fall when a strong wind blows; and, believe me, his constitution is bad; his brain is weak;

you will see it well enough; the poor man has visions continually; how long can this state last? and how will it end?"

Although I was exasperated to the utmost at this evidence of want of filial feeling, I still endeavoured to restrain myself; for the present I did not wish to make him my personal enemy, although he had long been considered as such in my heart, and I answered therefore calmly but very seriously,—

"Ah! yes, we must not lose all hope; I cannot rejoice you by speaking of any great or *certain* hope, but I need not distress you by any overwhelming anxiety; for first of all, before I can venture to give any decided opinion, we must wait for the effects of the remedies employed."

"Of course — of course;" and rising from his chair, Lord Mortimer walked up and down the room, with his arms folded and his head bent down, as if reflecting on some serious matter.

"Have you not inquired the cause of his illness?" he asked suddenly in a sly way, and remained standing before me apparently with careless indifference. But I was sufficiently prepared to understand the violent feelings which contended with each other in his heart, and which with difficulty he concealed beneath apparent calmness.

"No, sir; but I should think that anxiety and sorrow, old age and his peculiar mode of living, are quite sufficient to account for such an illness."

THE MADMAN OF ST. JAMES'.

"So it is, particularly the latter, I mean," interrupted he hastily; "pay especial attention to that; it is not sorrow or anxiety, for he has always led a life of pleasure. No, it is old age, and his mode of life. Oh! I see it plainly enough;—but—we must speak still further on the subject. I wish now only to take you to my friends, who are waiting for me below—come now."

"I have dined, my lord!" I said.

"Bah!—well—we must not let you starve;—but not with us—to sit alone at table is but stupid work. We must drink, and play, and hunt, to pass away the time. What is there else in life but *ennui?*" and half by force he drew me with him down stairs.

Reader, that was Lord Mortimer; you know him now from one side. Well, patience! you shall soon learn to know him from another.

We entered the dining-room. The three guests were sitting or rather lying at the table in their red hunting coats, their caps on, and their feet put upon the sofas which were drawn to the table; they greeted me with a most fashionable nod of recognition, when I had the honour of being introduced by our crimson host.

"Well, how is the old one, eh?" asked one of them, a baronet out of the neighbourhood.

"Why, the doctor is satisfied beyond measure; are you not?" answered the feeling son, with a sarcastic look which was intended to express his delight.

"*Not* beyond measure," I remarked; "but still tolerably satisfied."

"And are *you?*" whispered one of the guests to Mortimer.

Mortimer gave him a very intelligible wink, and said,—

"William! fresh bottles and glasses—Burgundy!"

The wine was brought, the glasses were filled and emptied; the more they drank, the more noisy and unrestrained became their conversation, the more ringing their laughter, as if there were no sick person, or, as Mortimer believed, one on the point of death, in that house. And yet his son could have such a carouse! At first the chase and its adventures were discussed; then, as is usually the case with young people, when the wine has done its work, love matters had their turn, and at the expense of each other they laughed, and drank, and wagered.

But after some time the conversation thus forced upon me became tedious, and I was already thinking in what manner I could manage to get away, when suddenly it took a turn which not only engaged my whole attention, but was of the greatest interest for me with regard to the matter I had in hand, although it did not throw much light on it.

Of all those present Lord Mortimer was the merriest, almost the loudest; but still it did not escape my quiet observation that behind this mirth he was endeavouring to conceal a troubled spirit, something that disturbed his most secret thoughts; for, as it appeared to me, he often sank into a peculiar dreamy state, and seemed lost to all that was going on around him; from this he was again aroused by the jokes of his noisy guests, and animated into taking part in them. It was in one of his gloomy moments that the baronet already mentioned called out,—

"Look at Mortimer; does he not look blooming to-day, like a rose?"

"Just so," exclaimed the one who was opposite, between him and me. "Just as the cheeks of the girl would bloom, if she had not escaped him again. I say, that is a desperate long chase!" And with these words, he threw a sly look at his friend, whilst pointing with a motion of his head to Mortimer.

Mortimer's bronzed face became red as crimson on hearing these words; and looking at the speaker with no particularly friendly expression of face, he remarked sullenly,—

"No personal joke, gentlemen, if you please; touch no sore point. You put me in mind, Gladstone, of the most serious adventure of my life; but this I swear to you: let the new-made Sir Robert Graham have either sold or let the estate he has just got—let him be where he may, into whatever hole or corner of the earth he has crept, I will find him notwithstanding his eternal changes of residence, and will

THE MADMAN OF ST. JAMES'.

have the girl, after all, in spite of all the devils who protect her!"

"That was a dangerous oath, Mortimer," said the baronet; "do not forget it, otherwise it will fall back on your own conscience."

"Well, that would not do him much harm," whispered my neighbour; "it would find some queer company there."

"Bah!" exclaimed the one who had been silent until now; "bah! a girl and a conscience!"

"Silence!" cried Mortimer himself. "We weary the good doctor; I can see it in his face."

"Pray do not leave off on my account, sir," said I, bowing. "I have also lived in the world, and from hearsay, at least, am acquainted with these kinds of things."

"But do just listen, Mortimer," began the baronet again; "if I were in your place—if, as you have often told me, you cannot live without this girl, and it is the object of your life to find her out, why don't you go after her, and end the whole affair at once?"

"Once again, silence, gentlemen!" answered Mortimer angrily; "none of you know how near at last I am to her, and what I alone know about her. Do you think I have only two arms, and those only the length of the arm of a human being? Ho! ho! that were bad. But that is not the case. I cannot—I cannot leave just now."

"Why not? Lord Seymour would be taken care

THE MADMAN OF ST. JAMES'. 203

of; the doctor is here, and what can you wish for more?"

I raised my eyes in the greatest suspense to Lord Mortimer's face: his head rested on his hands, which for a moment he had placed on the table.

"No, that won't do," whispered my neighbour again; "that is a bad affair. What do you think of it? Lord Mortimer is sitting at the present moment before the holes of two foxes, and it is well known that a man can only look in one direction at once."

"How, what do you mean?"

"What, don't you understand it then? One fox is sitting here at home, a valuable prey, and that one he wants to have—ha! ha!—and a vixen is doubling in another cover, and that one he won't lose."

"Ah!" thought I, while all the others broke out into a loud laugh, which Lord Mortimer was obliged to bear quietly, "if you only knew that it is just the same case with me at the present moment! But I will have the fox, the vixen, and the hunter besides."

"Well, now, what can he want here now?" asked the baronet, pretty loudly; "I thought the matter of the inheritance was settled."

With a haughty look Lord Mortimer left his chair, and throwing on the baronet a glance such as I should never have endured, he was just going to make some reply, when a servant entered the room with candles, and requested that I would go to the marquis, who, he said, had already asked for me several times.

"You will excuse me, gentlemen," said I, rising, and bowing to them.

"Wait, wait, doctor; I will go with you," said Lord Mortimer. Then, turning to his guests, he added, stammeringly,—

"Make yourselves at home, my friends, while I am away; we will soon be back, and then for a rubber."

With these words he took me by the arm, upon which he leaned heavily as we ascended the stairs, for he had drunk deeply, and his legs were at best quite as heavy as his tongue.

By this time it was evening, and darkness, increased by a slight mist, reigned around. The polished lamps burned brightly in the corridor through which we passed, and with the exception of the loud laughing and talking which proceeded from Lord Mortimer's drinking room, and was heard through half the house, such deep silence pervaded the dismal place, that our footsteps over the carpet appeared to me like the gliding of some nightly spirit.

Forgetting for the moment that the marquis had changed his apartment, we both proceeded to the room he had occupied until the afternoon of this day. Lord Mortimer opened the door, but with a half-uttered cry he started back on looking in, and finding it dark and unoccupied.

"Ha! ha!" said he, smiling at himself, "I thought —I thought—he was—but he is only—moved into another—come, come!—but the devil! is nobody here? Hallo! Paul, Paul!"

The steward, hearing this loud cry, hurried up to us, breathless with haste. The old man had not forgotten the undeserved chastisement of the morning, and knew the passionate temper of his future master. Holding his hand to his forehead, on which a red stripe was visible, he stammered out,—

"What is your pleasure, Lord Mortimer?"

"Where is the marquis, rascal, eh? and where have you and the other rascals been hiding yourselves?"

"We were waiting for you before his lordship's door, sir."

"Show us the way, and waste no more words."

The steward walked on before us. We descended one staircase, and then ascended another, while Lord Mortimer whistled a hunting song; and we then saw several servants standing before their master's door. They looked uneasy when they saw the state in which Lord Mortimer was, for probably they did not expect, as he had visitors, that he would appear again that day at the sick bed of his father.

But Lord Mortimer seemed to have made up his mind to remain with me there, and his servants were somewhat astonished when they saw their "rising sun" staggering rather heavily up with me.

"What are you doing here, scoundrels?"

No one dared to answer: they looked frightened at each other in silence.

"Up! stand before *my* room, you donkeys! one is enough here."

And the servants all crept slowly away, with the exception of one, who remained standing before the door.

We now entered the newly-arranged apartment of the marquis. The old steward preceded us, and opened the door, as usual, very gently.

The room looked quite cheerful, and produced a far more agreeable impression than the one in which I had found my patient on my arrival. It had white curtains, the large mirrors were all uncovered, paintings hung on the walls, which were covered with light-blue silk damask; only the dark carpet was the same, or at least one very like it. The chimney-place was of white marble, and in the ornamented grate the coals were still burning; and from the ceiling was suspended a lamp, which shed a mild but agreeable light throughout the whole of the large apartment.

"Ah, good evening, sir! Good evening, Mortimer!" said the marquis, when we entered.

"Good evening," answered Mortimer roughly, walking to the fireplace, where he began to knock about the coals noisily and stir up the fire, as if he

THE MADMAN OF ST. JAMES'. 207

wished to have something to do at a distance from his father.

" Be quiet, Mortimer ; you frighten me with that poker. Do not make such a noise, and sit down — do sit down."

Mortimer quitted the fireplace, and threw himself into a corner of the sofa with such violence that it cracked again.

The marquis cast a timid and almost beseeching look on his tender-hearted and excellent son—his son, his heir! He, however, did not notice it in the least, but stretched himself, and lounged about, looking around in every direction with astonishment.

" How do you find yourself, my lord ?" I asked, approaching the alarmed old man, who sat there cowering in his chair.

" Better, I think, sir. Thank you, thank you. You are a wonderful man. Just see what a deep breath I can draw. A————h! And I am tired too. The air really seems better here, if there was only no light."

" You will gradually accustom yourself to it, my lord," said I, taking his hand, which was less icy cold, and the pulse satisfied me.

" They have been bleeding you, eh ?" almost screamed Mortimer, who could not forget that he had just left the drinking party, and who did not seem to care that his sick father shrank together, terrified at his loud words.

THE MADMAN OF ST. JAMES'.

"Be quiet, be quiet, Mortimer," said the old man; "you frighten me every moment with your noise. You have visitors, I hear. Do go to them. The doctor will stay with me; will you not, sir?"

I bowed in silence.

"If the doctor stays, I stay too," said Mortimer yawning; "he must drink with us; he has not come here to fill the place of a sick-nurse."

"Well, then, if you like, take him with you to-day; but to-morrow he is mine."

"To-morrow is hunting, fox-hunting, and he is going out with us."

I now thought it was high time to speak for myself, and I therefore remarked, politely, but decidedly, "I thank you, sir, I thank you very much; but I shall neither drink nor play to-night, because I never play, and do not like to drink; neither shall I hunt to-morrow; because, if my visit here gives me nothing else to do, more important business requires my presence in another place."

Lord Mortimer looked at me sullenly in silence, and then tried to make himself still more comfortable on his sofa, by placing both feet on a chair which was standing close by him, and which he almost threw down by drawing it violently towards him.

"Now, this is kind of you," said the marquis, with a grateful look; "but you must not go away yet." And, with his hand, he made me a sign which nobody but myself saw, but which I at once understood.

THE MADMAN OF ST. JAMES'. 209

A pause now ensued, during which Mortimer whistled a hunting song. The old steward looked at me askance. I nodded to him, and remained seated, waiting in silence for what was to follow.

"Who sleeps in my room to-night?" asked the marquis, turning to Paul. "Whoever he may be, he will be able to sleep. I am tired."

"Charles will sleep here to-night, it is his turn," replied the steward; "shall I call him?"

"No, no, I won't have him; he snores, and that is dreadful; for then I not only see, but I hear also."

He was silent, and, with a ghastly expression on his frozen features, he looked at us one after the other.

"Now we have got it," muttered Mortimer; "the vision is coming back again. Oh, the doctor, the learned doctor!"

"Who spoke then?" exclaimed the terrified father, starting. "Say, who spoke then?"

"It is I, Mortimer, your lordship's son," cried out Mortimer, in a loud voice. "He is already dreaming with his eyes open," added he, in a low voice to me.

"Oh, I thought—go, do go, Mortimer, go, I beg you—my son! my son!" And he heaved a sigh, which sounded through the room like the whisper of a hovering spirit.

Another dreadful pause ensued; each looked at the other. Mortimer's face wore a threatening expression; that of the marquis was convulsively dis-

VOL. II.   P

210 THE MADMAN OF ST. JAMES'.

torted; the steward's mouth was wide open from fright, and with an expressive gesture he pointed to the sick man, who, gradually sinking back, appeared to be going to sleep; at last he closed his eyes; perhaps he resigned himself helplessly and half fainting to the overpowering influence of his own imagination.

The silence continued, and with it the horror of that night's scene.

" He is asleep," said Mortimer, smiling, and rising from his chair; " let us go away, that we may not awake him."

And taking me by the arm, he half drew me by force out of the room.

" *I* shall stop here to-night," whispered the steward, " and if anything happens —— "

" Then call me! Good night! "

We went out. I carried my point, and retired to my own room, and Mortimer returned to his carouse.

It was long past midnight when I still heard the laughing and noise of the wild guests.

CHAPTER X.

THE DOUBLE WILL.

I FOUND no quiet rest in my lonely room; a thousand fresh thoughts, occasioned by the unexpected events of the day, crowded on my mind, and in some degree confused the clear perception of things which I had preserved until now.

" But all will become clear to me," said I, by way of consoling myself;—"what I shall have to do next, whether I shall act immediately, or wait for what may happen. Well, to-morrow will come, and for to-day I have heard and seen enough to know, at least, that I am on the right track."

Encouraging myself in this manner, I lay down, but at first it was impossible for me to go to sleep; and when at last I had arrived at some degree of composure, dream after dream passed through my excited mind, so that I seemed to live over again all that had happened, and to see beforehand all that was to come.

But in all my dreams and visions no object stood so vividly before my imagination as Percy. His tall and commanding form hovered before me, always beckoning with its hand for me to come onwards, onwards; and when I was even fast asleep, I still seemed to myself continually to be chased onwards, and with all my efforts not to be able to keep back; for the power which urged me on was like the irresistible force of the storm which chases the clouds.

A hand seized me;—I started up, and followed out my dream in a half-waking state. Whose hand was it that seized me? Percy's hand alone it could and must be which restrained me in my hurried course; and just as it happens that, when arrived at the highest point of interest in a dream, knowing no longer how to resist or what to do, we loudly call on the name of the one who causes our anxiety, or who so entirely engrosses our thoughts, so I now called out with a loud voice,—

" Percy!—here—here—I am here!"

It was my own voice that now completely roused me. I opened my eyes, and perceived a pale face bending over me, full of astonishment and terror.

It was that of the old steward, who, holding a light in his hand, was standing by my bedside.

" What is the matter, Paul?" I asked, when I had recovered from the alarm which I felt at being thus roused from my dream.

" Heavens, sir!—what did you say just now?"

" What did I say?"

" Did you not say, ' Percy—Percy ' ? "

THE MADMAN OF ST. JAMES'.

"Did I say that?—and why should I not? I dare say I was dreaming."

"Yes, yes, sir—I believe it."

"And what do you want of me?"

The old man stood immoveable, still gazing at me in astonishment. He seemed to be reflecting what he had wished to say to me.

"Yes, what I wanted! Oh, yes, sir! I wanted to ask your pardon for disturbing you, but will you please to come up to my lord? He has just got a fit, I think;—perhaps you could help him."

"And is Mortimer with him?—Lord Mortimer, I mean," and immediately corrected myself.

"No, sir, he is asleep! His visitors only left half an hour ago, and his servants have just taken him to bed. He sleeps the dead sleep of the drunken;—he cannot be waked again to-day."

"And the sleep of a good conscience," thought I; and I quickly dressed myself.

Often in my life had I been awakened in the night to attend a patient, but never had I attended such a summons with so much alacrity as now. The power which urged me onwards in my dream seemed to influence me even now, and I followed it willingly, full of hope, to which I was not able to give a name. Percy's fate had never been so near my heart, never had my mind been so full of the wish of reinstating him in his rights, as on this night, when, stealing through the empty house of his fathers, I was on my way to the

214   THE MADMAN OF ST. JAMES'.

sick bed of him who, with a curse for a portion, had closed his doors against him, and driven him forth into the cold world.

We entered the chamber of the marquis. He lay, as usual, in his arm-chair, his head fallen back, and his eyes open, but vacantly fixed on the ceiling. We made but little noise in entering, but he started at it; his senses appeared to be extremely acute and easily roused.

"Who is there?" he muttered between his teeth.

"It is I, my lord."

"Who?"

"I, the doctor—your confidant."

"And who are you?" he asked, looking at the old steward.

"I? why, I am your lordship's servant, Paul."

"Ha! that is right; then you are both there. You are strong—you can help me. I am so weak, opposed to him—to him!"

"What is the matter with you, my lord?" I asked, sympathisingly, taking his cold, damp hand, which immediately clasped mine firmly, as if he would not lose again the support he had just obtained. "Against whom shall we defend you?"

He gave me a look I shall never forget; it was so piteous, so helpless, so broken-hearted, that, firm as I was, I involuntarily shuddered.

"He will—kill me!" he gasped out, with difficulty.

"Kill you?—who?"

"Percy!" shrieked he, in such a loud voice that it echoed through the whole room, and old Paul started up in a fright. This was the second time that night he had thus unexpectedly heard this name.

"Percy?" I asked, softly, trembling inwardly.

"Ha! he does not know it—you do not know it, and I thought you knew it."

The steward shook his grey head, and looked on me piteously. I was already on the point of discovering myself—of divulging everything—but I still hesitated. I must find out a little more, and have some forbearance and consideration for the health of him who had been confided to my care.

"Who is Percy?" I therefore asked.

The old man raised himself suddenly, looked at me inquiringly, but kindly, and then, trying to smile, he said,—

"Ah! it is my son—yes!"

"And he wished to kill you?—why, then?"

"Because he is dead," he groaned.

"Ha! ha!" thought I, "is that it?—forwards, Percy!—Because he is dead he will destroy you!—Oh! do the dead kill the living? that is not possible, my lord—perfectly impossible!"

"Yes! but he kills me, because I—I have murdered him!"

"That is not true, my lord," stammered out the steward, "your lordship has *not* destroyed him."

216   THE MADMAN OF ST. JAMES'.

"*Not?*—have I *not?* I thought I had. Where is he, then?"

I collected myself. I motioned to old Paul with my hand that he should be silent, and then said, firmly and solemnly,—

"No, my lord, you have *not!* Percy, your son Percy, lives!"

"He lives? ha! how you do know that?"

"I read it, my lord!"

"Reading again! and on my face? eh?—does my face say, too, that I have not destroyed him? Why, that is a capital face! ha! ha! but *I* see dreadful faces!" And his eyes remained fixed on the vacant space before him. I pressed his hand tighter, to withdraw him from this dreamy state, for I wished gradually to lead him onward to the truth, without forcing it.

"Listen to me, my lord—look at me! Believe me, in truth you have not destroyed him. He lives!"

"He lives!—ah! but he hates me!"

"Not that either. No! he loves you; he prays for you!"

The old steward now stared at me, and seemed almost as full of astonishment as the marquis. Both looked like stone statues; their eyes hung on my lips, and the solemn stillness which at this moment reigned around us was as deep as if there had been nothing living in the room.

THE MADMAN OF ST. JAMES'. 217

"He loves me—he prays for me!" cried the old man, suddenly wringing his hands; "then I shall go mad—then I must go mad. Death for death; blood for blood!" And he sank back, as if lifeless, in his chair.

"Bring some cold water and towels, Paul," I said to the steward, who was still standing there in speechless amazement, not knowing if he should believe my words or not.

"Quick, quick, Paul; we must not say any more, for to-day it is enough."

The man quickly fetched what I required; we put some cold wet bandages round the head of the patient, who sat there without making the least opposition; and then I gave him a composing draught out of my travelling medicine chest.

We said nothing more; he remained passive in our hands, and allowed us to do with him what we judged best. He only still held my hand tight—tighter still. The night gradually passed; the first rosy light of morning slowly pierced into that darkened room; he still held my hand. At last he gently relinquished his hold—the convulsive agitation which had been on his face disappeared; he had fallen asleep. With a look at the steward, I pointed to him,—"Breathe not a word of what we have spoken about, and what you have heard from me," said I, in a low voice; "nobody must know it—not even he himself when he awakes; we must see what effect it has. You understand me, Paul, do you not?"

"I know it all, sir,—all. Ah! heavens! yes, I shall obey you."

And I returned to my room, almost exhausted from the suspense in which my mind had been kept.

"It is going on well," said I to myself when I was alone. "But am I working here, or is Providence at work for me? It is Providence, Providence, —an all-wise Providence has worked before me in this man's heart, and what I have to do is but a mere trifle."

I felt in my heart that I was the weak but willing instrument in His Almighty hand, and with that I was contented.

"Percy," said I gently, when I lay down to rest, "Percy, we can now sleep in peace; all is going on well!"

At an early hour the following morning, even before I had paid my first visit to the marquis, Lord Mortimer again appeared in my room, dressed for hunting. The effects of the excesses of the previous evening were but half slept off, and were still very evident on his unpleasing features. He looked paler and older than usual, his temper was morose, as is generally the case after such excess. After he had coldly and hastily wished me good morning, he addressed me in the following words:—

THE MADMAN OF ST. JAMES'. 219

"You see we are now ready for hunting; I have come to fetch you. Dress yourself quickly, and follow me."

"It cannot be your wish, Lord Mortimer, to make me faithless to my most sacred duties, especially as, in fulfilling my own, I fulfil yours also. Yesterday I refused your kind invitation, and to-day also I must again decline it. Leave me here; I am now more necessary than ever to the marquis."

"Well, then, if you will have it so; I almost expected it. You can serve me here too."

"Certainly, sir, that is my opinion also!"

"Yes, yes,—but understand me rightly—come, let us sit down familiarly together, for I have got a serious word to speak to you."

Lord Mortimer spoke these words,—the purport of which was evidently to deceive me,—to win my confidence, and denote his confidence in me; but the tone in which he spoke belied his words; they expressed nothing cordial, they were uttered coldly, I might say so domineeringly; so that, though the meaning was intended to be agreeable, they produced quite a contrary effect on me.

"Speak, I am listening!" I answered, and seated myself beside him on the sofa.

"Well, then, my dear doctor," he began, "if you prefer my father's company to mine, I can have no objection."

"Excuse me sir, it is not here a question of preference but of duty."

"Very well—*duty* then—you see I agree with you in every thing;—if, therefore, your duty detains you here,—with which I must be satisfied, since I cannot help myself,—I say you can still be of great service to me *here.*"

"With all my heart, Lord Mortimer; for that purpose I have come here."

"Let me speak out. Yesterday you must have ascertained perfectly well my father's state of health; do you still entertain great hopes?"

"Certainly not—but still some—some still ——"

"Very well; this time, believe me, it is all going downhill with him; the visions, the delusions get the upper hand, and return very often; he will soon have no intervals of rest—is it not so?—must we not expect this?"

"Unfortunately, yes, we must expect it!"

"Well, then—you see!—therefore—what must be done, and what I wish for, must take place before these intervals of rest cease."

"And what must take place, if I may be allowed to ask the question; what do you wish for?"

"You shall hear directly, doctor; here, I give you my hand on it that I mean honestly; only think—do you know—eh? that my father—will leave the world—without a will?"

I was astonished. What, had not this yet

THE MADMAN OF ST. JAMES'   221

been managed? But I concealed my surprise beneath an appearance of undivided attention, and answered simply,—

"I should have thought that would not have been necessary, as you are his lordship's only heir."

At these words I looked sharply in his face; but the man who was sitting beside me had a heart of iron, his countenance never changed.

"It is so—do not doubt it," he answered; "however, there are several cousins from a near branch of the family who have, more or less, some pretensions to my father's estates, and on account of these—you understand me?"

"If that is the case, a will certainly would be desirable for these cousins, whose welfare you take so warmly to heart, although I do not yet believe there is any immediate danger."

"Let us leave that now, we are speaking of the will; and now listen to what I am going to tell you. There *is one* certainly in existence which several years ago my father made in the presence of some lawyers, and which was signed by them. In that will there are legacies given to all our relations; but the chief point is—my father, either from caprice, or out of consideration for this or that relation, or even perhaps from a fear that his death might be accelerated thereby, as old people sometimes believe,—my father, I say, has never been able to make up his mind to sign this document, so important for us all, and will never

222   THE MADMAN OF ST. JAMES'.

do so until he himself believes that his last hour is
come. In case, therefore, he should die suddenly,
without having signed it, a general confusion would
take place—a rush here and there—continual ex-
planations, and Heaven knows what else besides would
be the consequence—and—I alone should thereby
have to sacrifice the most time, and have the most
trouble."

"Well?"

"You see, therefore, that, as far as regards me as the
rightful heir, and the one most interested, everything
depends upon the signature; and as you perhaps may
find an opportunity, and my father might even address
to you some question concerning it, it is my wish
that you should take advantage of the opportunity
afforded you to make him consent to sign it, and I
need hardly add that this most friendly service shall
not remain unacknowledged."

Ah! now I understood the whole beautifully-
planned scheme! I already began to have a notion
why the marquis had not as yet signed that paper.
He had not yet fully made up his mind; the wavering
between right and wrong wore him out, and kept him
back; it was so;—no other reason could be given
for it.

Without noticing the "acknowledgment" I was
to receive, which Lord Mortimer had been so kind
as to mention, I said,—

"But if he persists in not signing it?"

THE MADMAN OF ST. JAMES'. 223

"Well, then it will not be your fault. But still some persuasion from you might be of some use. Old age and illness have indeed made him more obstinate than he used to be, and therefore you must represent to him that this formal legal act is all the more immediately necessary. Take advantage of the right moment; address yourself to his conscience!— you understand me!"

Ha! and this shameless man dared to say all this to my face, and with the most careful and deliberate composure of manner. I should address myself to his father's conscience in his behalf! "Yes, yes," thought I, "that shall be done, and something else too!"

"And now what next?" I asked. "I see that you have not yet finished."

"Yes, indeed! one point still remains for us; the signature of my father must be witnessed and undersigned by a physician, with the distinct remark that he has written it voluntarily, and was at the time in his perfectly sound mind. You see therefore how necessary it is to have his signature as soon as possible."

"And who has arranged it thus?" I asked.

"Arranged it, sir? What do you mean? It is most desirable in this particular case. Do you not understand why? The cousins might come and say,— 'The signature is recent—signed to-day; but the will itself was of yesterday. *Yesterday* he was in his

224   THE MADMAN OF ST. JAMES'.

sound mind, but to-day he is *not*—we require *more* of you now.' Is that clear to you, doctor?"

"Oh, perfectly! You are right—and then?"

"Then, *you* sign it!"

And that was said to me so coolly, in such blind confidence, that I could hardly restrain the expression of my disgust, and with difficulty prevented myself from laughing in his face. Really, a pretty idea for me—that I—I, in favour of Lord Mortimer, and at the expense of Percy, should aid him by bearing witness to such a document.

"I shall not swerve a finger's breadth from my duty," was my reply; "I shall do everything I ought to do."

"That is right, doctor, quite right. I see—I see you understand my affairs,—and that is just what I wished. Yes, we understand each other."

"Yes, I know your intention; and you, my opinion!"

"Now, that satisfies me; and now, good morning."

"A pleasant morning, sir, and good sport."

"You should not tell me that, doctor; I can shoot nothing now; I hope your aim will be better."

"*I* always take aim at the right mark!"

"Ha! ha! But still one often misses, too!"

"I shall take extra pains this time!"

"That's right, that's right! Good morning."

"Good morning."

He went away; thinking, perhaps, he had left a

THE MADMAN OF ST. JAMES'. 225

blockhead behind him; and I remained behind, convinced that I had seen through a scoundrel.

Would he cheat me?—me, and still more his brother? Without doubt!—Would I cheat him? Is that cheating to take away from a rascal that which does not belong to him? Certainly not.—But had I a right to do it? Yes! for at this moment I stood here as the moral agent of Percy, and everything spoke in his favour;—my conscience, my feelings, my conviction, and, in addition to these, the law.

Now, for the first time, I knew what I could do, and what I had to do for Percy—the noble, right-minded, betrayed Percy. Everything depended on prudently guiding the marquis. If he required of me that which was right, I would do it with all my heart; if he did not require anything of me, I must then tell him what was right; and that I was determined to do, whatever might come of it. Never mind until the time come; "only go on, little Job! probe him even to the depths of his heart." God will help!

Hardly had I concluded this soliloquy, which gave a new spur to my resolutions, and a new direction to my hopes, when I heard a tap at my door, and the old steward appeared. An expression of unusual cheerfulness lay on his wrinkled face; for he seemed always sorrowful.

"He is gone, sir!" said he, in a peculiarly exulting tone.

VOL. II.   Q

226 THE MADMAN OF ST. JAMES'.

" Who is gone?"

" Lord Mortimer! And please, sir, do come up quickly; my lord can hardly wait until you get there."

" How long did he sleep?"

" Until an hour ago; he is quite cheerful. Oh! what did you tell him, sir?"

" What did I tell him, then?"

" What, sir! do you not remember it any longer? Oh!" cried the faithful old servant, raising his hands, while a tear trickled down his furrowed cheeks, " confess it, sir! Yes, yes, you know still much more—perhaps, you know everything."

" What do you mean by everything, old man? I do not understand you."

" No, sir, no—you need not dissemble with me. Why, when you came first, did I not feel as if at last an angel of peace had entered our melancholy house? Ah! and last night—you need not blush—you were just as much affected as he or I, when you spoke of Lord Percy."

" You take, then, some interest in him, eh?"

" What, sir! have not these arms carried that dear, good little Percy?"

" But those arms have, perhaps, carried Lord Mortimer also?"

" Yes, unfortunately they have; but who can see into the future? And both were the sons of the same father! Come, oh, come! he knows every-

THE MADMAN OF ST. JAMES'. 227

thing—he knows everything; it is just as if he had dreamed it. 'When Mortimer is gone,' said he, 'call him, and then go out; my heart has awoke from a long sleep; I must speak to some person—he must tell me everything, and I, too, must tell him much, very much.'"

"But how is it possible, this sudden change?"

"One spark, one single little spark, sir, and a whole barrel of gunpowder goes off! Ah! the many years, the many melancholy, comfortless years; and then that ever-pleading voice in my heart, and the remembrance of times gone by! And then you came! You were the kindling spark, for you said 'He loves you!' He would never believe that when I told him; and even the clergyman, Mr. Graham, he would not believe."

"Ah, Mr. Graham! Do you know him? Who is he?"

"Do I know him, and who is he? Do you not know that, then? I thought you knew everything."

"I know nothing, old man! I know nothing at all. Come, come—we will go."

The steward looked at me with an incredulous and bewildered look as we descended the stairs. Was it my fault that he had read my heart? His eyes were full of love, and the writing in my heart was clear and intelligible.

He remained standing before the door which he

q 2

228   THE MADMAN OF ST. JAMES'.

had opened for me, gave me once more a look of encouragement, and I entered the sick man's room alone.

The marquis sat, as usual, in his arm-chair, which he left neither day nor night.

"Come nearer; come quickly—nearer, sir," cried he, as soon as I entered. "I know your step already, and I am no longer frightened at it. Good morning, sir; good morning." And he extended to me the hand which the evening before I had held in mine trembling, and bathed in the damp sweat of anguish; but to-day it was warm, and I distinctly felt its almost friendly pressure, an honour his lordship very rarely bestowed.

"You find yourself well, my lord, do you not?"

"Well? oh no, not yet. But still I am better than I was yesterday. I have slept, and—dreamed; but not dreamed as usual."

"And what have you dreamed?"

"That *you* were with me, and that you told me a story; that you—ah! see how cheerfully the sun shines in!—that you—knew Percy—ah! how easy the name is to me now!—that you—you had seen him ——"

"No, really, my lord, that I did *not* tell you," I cried, involuntarily.

"No, I did not say *that*; I only said I dreamed it. But, sir, still that was a sweet—sweet dream!"

I was silent, and looked kindly and compassionately

upon him. I was not in the least embarrassed. I had thought of another plan as to how I should lead him on to Percy, which in his state of health appeared to me less exciting, but now he himself gave the direction I wished. I reflected a few moments as to how I could lead him to follow my ideas; but during that short season of reflection my face must have expressed something rather stern and determined, for the old man, who had been attentively observing me, put another construction on its expression: he suddenly became sorrowful, and said, in a low and melancholy voice,—

" Ah, then, it was only a dream, after all! and I am still very unhappy."

This was just what I wanted. I quickly questioned him, as usual, about his health, and was indeed most satisfied with the answers I received; but while speaking to him, the bright expression of confidence, joy— perhaps even of hope—which at my entrance had beamed so visibly upon his face, suddenly disappeared, and in its place a dark, gloomy cloud spread itself over his sunken features, giving them that melancholy, sorrowful, and at the same time uneasy and restless expression which his face presented on the entrance of a stranger. He sighed deeply, and fixed his usually restless eyes silently on the ceiling above him.

" Listen, sir," said he, suddenly, in a half-audible voice, and motioning with his hand that I should approach him still nearer; " do come for once quite close

230 THE MADMAN OF ST. JAMES'.

to me—so., I want to ask you, in confidence, a question, a silly question, which—which, I don't know why—has long tormented me, and which has just occurred to me again. Could a man—a healthy, strong young man"—he just gasped out—" could he, if he were confined among lunatics, lose his reason?"

Aha! he was going on his own way, and I could not get at him in the manner I wished. Well, never mind; I will meet him on this road too. Still, for a moment I was at a loss as to how I should answer this extraordinary question. The *truth* I dare not tell him; it might be attended with serious consequences. I therefore said, boldly and in a clear, loud voice,—

" No, my lord."

" Be quiet! not so loud, sir—not so loud; nobody else need hear it. *No*, you say—really *not?* That is well—that is very, very well. Answer further. Have you ever been with Sir John —— in Bethlehem Hospital?"

" Yes," I replied, " I have very often been there with him."

" And is it not very dreadful there?" And his anxious eyes, as he asked this question, stared at me like those of an idiot; for life or death lay for him in my reply.

" No, my lord, it is not dreadful; the unhappy are consoled, and the sick are cured; *that* is not dreadful."

"Really, really? — they are consoled, you say? That is beautiful!   Oh!" ——

And he sighed deeply.   My reply had seemingly relieved him with respect to something, but only to something; for another question seemed to hover on his lips, but perhaps it would have cost him a great, and, in his state of health, too great an effort to utter it.   Therefore I resumed,—

"But I have also been in other lunatic asylums in England which please me even better than Bethlehem Hospital."

"Which, which?" he asked, with a quivering lip.

I named to him several I knew, but still I saw no change in the expression of his face, although his eyes hung on my lips with the most intense anxiety. Then I added quickly, somewhat softly, "I have also been in St. James', in the county of ——."

"What?" he cried loudly, starting up as if a flash of lightning had struck him.

I already repented having spoken that word, but now he again appeared to recover himself.   He clasped his hands, pressed them together to his heart, and then, bending down his head, he muttered something, which, however, I could not understand.

"You have been *there?*" he at length stammered out.

"Yes, my lord.   I remained there some time.   Do you know it also?"

"No, no!   I do not know it," he almost shrieked

out. "Do not ask me. Do *you* know anybody there?"

"I know several there—Mr. Elliotson, the director —— "

"Ah! yes—well?"

"Mr. Lorenz, the superintendent-physician;" and I named to him all the names I knew of the officials there.

"There are many patients and many unhappy people there, eh?"

"Very many, my lord."

"Do you know anything of them?" he gasped out, with the greatest difficulty, and in a voice scarcely intelligible. "I mean any of those—of those unhappy ones?"

"Oh, yes! I knew many. A colonel of the name of Lincoln, if I am not mistaken; a baronet, Sir Charles ——; a painter, Mr. Kingston; an actor, Mr. Bateman."

"Nobody else? No young man? Ah! be merciful, though I was not merciful to him! A young man, I say,—tall, handsome—oh, my God!"

"Oh, yes!" I answered, as if suddenly recollecting myself—"Mr. Brown, a handsome, excellent young man; I believe he was an architect."

"No, no!" cried the old man, with a countenance of contrition and despair; "you do *not* know him —you do not know him—you have never been there!"

"But I *have* been there, my lord," I exclaimed; "on my word I have been there!" and to put an end to this painful scene I added,—

"If you would only tell me the name?"

"Ah, the name! Come here—closer—quite close! Do you not know? Did you not see? Be quiet— Mortimer is not here? Mr.—Mr. Sid—— "

"Sidney!" I said. "Yes, I know *him* very well."

Hardly, however had the name escaped my lips, when I heard him call out loudly. He sank back, a deathlike paleness overspread his face, but only for a moment; then I heard an unusual sound—sobbing, loud sobbing. He extended his hands towards me; they clasped me, they drew me towards him, even to his breast. I stood bent over him, he drew my head to his shoulder, tears ran down his cheeks, he wept aloud.

Thus passed several minutes. Then, drying his tears, in quite an altered voice, and smiling calmly, he said to me,—

"Oh, why did you not tell me before that you knew my—my Percy?"

"My lord! how could I venture—how could I hope?"

"Why not, why not? Did he not then say anything to you about me? No message? Not a word?"

"Ah, my lord, did I not tell you even yesterday

234 THE MADMAN OF ST. JAMES'.

that he loves you, he prays for you? Was that not sufficiently intelligible?"

"It is well, sir—it is well! Do not speak! I see you know all,—you know how I have acted. That dreadful deed, you know that; but not my unfortunate character, and how I came to act thus. Now, I alone must speak—I only. Do not interrupt me before I have finished my unhappy history, for I also have one to tell you, and you shall judge from my sincerity if I mean honestly by you and by myself. There, there, sit down; but keep hold of my hand, and if you feel any disgust towards me, then draw yours away. Ha! I have been a great sinner, but God will still give me strength to confess all before I die, and you—*you* shall be my confessor."

I seated myself close beside him; and in his broken manner of speaking, I listened to the following extraordinary self-accusation :—

"I was a proud man—a headstrong, passionate man. I have never loved a woman; and that—that is the hardest thing I can ever say of myself. About twenty-nine years ago—I was then already forty-one years of age—I saw a young girl of eighteen, the daughter of the Viscount of Dunsdale—ha! and for the first time in my life a passion seized me—a headlong, burning passion, which clouded my reason for a time, and reduced me to the level of a brute; for the later such a passion comes, the more violent and unnatural it is. Oh! what I did, sir, suffer me to

THE MADMAN OF ST. JAMES'. 235

pass *that* over in silence—I wish it could be for ever buried and forgotten. But I was too proud, too despicably proud, to make her my wife, for never in any way would I submit to any control; but I was *compelled* to do it—compelled by her relations, by my own relations—compelled by the voice of the world. It was the first time I had endured compulsion, and it was enough to kindle in me the ardent thirst for vengeance. And I did revenge myself—on Percy, my eldest son! On him, from the hour of his birth, I vented the greater part of my fury: the remainder I reserved for his mother. To me he was the living reproach of my unworthy conduct; in him I hated myself, for he was the cause of my pride being humbled, the cause of the bondage to which I had been compelled to submit, and which now I could never shake from me. I detested him even as I detested her who, against my wish, had given him life. I never could see him but with aversion and disgust for myself, so I sent him away out of my sight;—I cast him from me, just as we would cast off a scorpion which has wounded us, and poisoned our heart's blood. But—but Providence is just, and uses the same means to punish us as we have dared to use to insult its justice. Do not be surprised, but despise me. Notwithstanding my aversion, once more I became the miserable slave of my blind passion. This time, however, no one could compel me to take her for my wife, for she was already my wife,

236   THE MADMAN OF ST. JAMES'.

and became the mother of my second son. But
Mortimer was not hateful to me; his birth had not
humbled me, and in my eyes he was my only son.
I wished to make up to him all that in my blind
belief nature and Percy had done amiss to me. I
therefore loved this Mortimer without bounds. But,
sir, what more shall I tell you of myself? I have
nearly finished, for all that remains still untold was
but the consequence of this unworthy love, founded
alike on hatred, and injustice, and crime. This Mortimer was a rogue; he flattered me, he deceived me;
he governed and misled me by his flattery, and—and
I determined he alone should be my heir. Then
Percy came to me—Percy, whom I hated—Percy,
whom I could not see without aversion and self-
reproach,—and—and I was cruel towards him, the
innocent cause of this hatred. I drove him away
from me! And then came Mortimer to me, and
said, 'Percy does not only despise your commands,
and your intentions towards me, your heir; Percy is
not only a disobedient son; no! Percy will bring a
stain on your proud name; he will take for his wife
a poor girl of no family, and thus contaminate your
pure blood, and disgrace your name. You see now
what Percy is!—learn at last to know your son;
and if you will prevent all this, prevent it at once;
otherwise he will compel you to do just as he likes.
See, I will support you. I know a good school for
him, for your dear son Percy is gone mad.'

THE MADMAN OF ST. JAMES'. 237

"'That he is,' cried I, in my passion; 'he is mad, and shall suffer for it. He shall expiate all for me, and for himself also; and I will cast off all thought of him from my mind. Go, and treat him as if he were a madman.'

"And *he did* treat him as if he were a madman, and I permitted him to do it; still more, I, his own father, urged him on to do it. Then it became all like night to me. Ah! Graham has often said that God would punish me,—that, although I was a rich and powerful nobleman, God had still more power than I. I laughed at him, for I believe I was mad myself from rage; but he would not leave off, this Graham. Just as he did before, when he and old Paul opposed the settlement of the will which was against all that was lawful and right, just so he opposed me now. He even went one morning so far as to threaten me, this Graham! but I then showed him the door, and insulted him, as I had insulted Percy, and he went—he went, and I have never seen him again."

"But the will?" I asked, trembling.

"Yes, the will—thank God! I once had a reasonable hour—to this Graham I owed it—and I caused *two* wills to be drawn up, one in favour of Mortimer, and one in favour of Percy; for the lawyers would have it thus, and I saw that it was best to have a hole through which I might escape, if God should prove stronger than I: and may He bless

Graham for it! these two wills I still have by me, and neither signed!"

I was speechless with astonishment—with emotion —with anger; a thousand feelings contended in my breast; this noble Graham! this miserable father! He then continued :—

"Now—now, however, the moment is come. God is here and *is* stronger than I am, and He has made me feel it. I will sign, and you—*you* shall be my witness! here, here," cried he, almost breathless; "quick—we are alone—here, here is the key!"

And he tore a small key from a ribbon which hung round his neck.

"Yonder cabinet there; unlock it—so—so—that is right; it must be in the drawer on the left—so— right, right, give it me!"

I gave him a small packet of papers, at the top of which was the will in favour of Mortimer.

"Give me the pen there," continued he eagerly; "and push the table towards me; so, so, that will do."

And I pushed the table forward, and gave him the pen; and, with a hasty trembling hand, he wrote his name, and his title, and the date of the day under the writing.

"What are you doing? what are you doing?" I exclaimed, terrified; "that is the will in favour of Mortimer!"

"Sir," answered he very calmly, "do you think I

THE MADMAN OF ST. JAMES'. 239

do not know what I am doing? so much sense I have
still left, and you will see; and you—you sign too,
and add the remark also that I do this voluntarily,
and am in my perfect and sound mind, for thus will
my dear son Mortimer have it."

"No," I exclaimed, "never will I do that; that
would be a shameful deception."

The marquis looked at me with an expression of
extreme surprise;—he even seemed disposed to smile
at this fearful moment; his hand pointed with
authority to the paper I held in mine, and for the
first time I remarked a beaming, triumphant expression in his usually lustreless eyes.

"Write," he said, "write, and with courage. God
sees what I am doing, and what you are doing;—for
He is not far from me now!"

I understood him; I believed, at least, I understood
him; and I signed the paper as Mortimer and his
father wished it to be signed.

When I had finished, I handed it to him; he held
it in his hand and silently examined it; with a joyful
look he glanced rapidly over it. Suddenly the door
opened, and, pale and breathless, the old steward
entered.

"Stop, my lord; he comes—Lord Mortimer, I
mean; he has just dismounted!"

The aged father looked up to heaven; his smile
was radiant, benign, as if under some holy influence;

240 THE MADMAN OF ST. JAMES'.

he spoke no other word than " God has sent him; I will deceive him, just as he has a hundred times deceived me."

At this moment Mortimer entered; when he saw the expression of our faces, he involuntarily coloured up; with a rapid look he glanced about him, and then remained standing, and said,—

" Well, what has happened, then? Why do you look so astonished at me?"

" Mortimer!" cried the father, in a shrill voice that pierced my heart like a knife; " Mortimer! see here; my will!"

More he could not say; the mental excitement which had supported him so long was over, and, like a broken reed, he sank back in his chair; his former fear and timidity again seized him.

Trembling with terror and anxiety lest he should breathe his last in this dreadful moment, I hurried up to him.

But Mortimer—the happy Mortimer, holding in his hand that important document, had only one feeling, and this feeling was easy enough to be read in his savage face. It was a feeling of delight and intoxicating triumph to see at last the necessary form completed for the sake of which he had committed so many crimes, the reward of which he had not believed to be so near at hand.

Yet how great and well calculated is God's almighty wisdom! He may bestow strength and cunning on the bad man to plan and execute his crimes, but He withholds from him the clear honest judgment of the good man, who is aware at the right moment of the change in his fate, and stops in his course when he sees the abyss of perdition open before him. He strikes him with blindness, when he requires to be most clear-sighted in the recognition of his errors; once carried away by his passion, he does not stop until he has arrived at the end of his mortal career, and sees it is too late to turn back.

Had Mortimer in his blind presumption understood how to decipher aright our terrified faces, when he, at this important moment, thus suddenly and unexpectedly appeared before us, he would have done something else than rejoice; but he overlooked in his certain victory the most important point; he forgot to prove that he deserved the confidence of his ill-used father, and his own deserts; he thought only of the will; and he smiled, and rejoiced, and was quite satisfied with himself.

I still stood there, horror-struck at the events which had just happened. I trembled with suspense; for, although from outward appearances I still had cause for doubt, yet my heart felt none, but believed firmly that something else would soon take place to make all sure.

And this "something" did take place. Hardly was Mortimer gone out (the steward, terrified and anxious, remained in the room), when Lord Seymour

VOL. II.

recovered his senses and raised himself in his chair.

"Is he gone?" he whispered, looking around him.

"Yes, my lord, yes—he is gone!"

"Then—quick—quick, lock—lock the door—so. And now there, there," he continued, tearing from my hand the paper I had taken up, and giving it to the old steward, "away—away with it—there—in the fire—in the fire."

The steward looked at his master, then at me, and then again at the will. The most important moment in Mortimer's life was come, and it passed as quickly as all such moments do in this life; for the steward, with a step as firm as the knowledge of doing a good action could make it, went to the fireplace, his head turned toward his master, and his arm with the paper stretched out before him; thus he approached the fire, which, blazing and crackling, roared in the old chimney.

Still a look, still a pause, and a sign from the eye of his master, which was intently fixed on him, and he threw the paper on the glowing coals, as one would throw away with disgust something polluting.

In one moment noiselessly and quickly the flames had seized the paper and consumed it, and in another short moment a puff of smoke rose high above the flames. Thus perished the whole happiness and joy of Lord Mortimer, who had lately left that room in all the flush and pride of triumph.

THE MADMAN OF ST. JAMES'. 243

We stood there, silent and agitated; a deep sigh relieved our oppressed hearts, and it sounded like the death-knell of the many hopes just crushed for ever. We still looked at the greedily-devouring flames, which, after having done their work of destruction, quietly flickered over the coals as if they had consumed only a common bit of waste-paper.

The marquis was the first to break silence.

"And now, Paul, here is the key!" And again he took a key from his bosom, and gave it to the old servant, who received it with trembling hands. "Open it—unlock it—behind me—in the chair—you know, you know."

As quickly as his agitation would allow, Paul did as he was told, and at length drew out a will, exactly like the one just destroyed, from a secret drawer concealed in the arm-chair, upon which the marquis, like a hen over her brood, had sat day and night. He gave it to him; it was the will in favour of the first-born son, Percy.

"The pen!" cried he.

He took the pen and signed it; then he handed the paper to me; I wrote under his name the same words I had written on the other.

"And now, Paul, you—you sign it too; you are our witness."

Paul took the paper and pen, trembling with joy and fear, and undersigned the will as witness. The work was completed, and Percy declared to be

244   THE MADMAN OF ST. JAMES'.

the indisputable and acknowledged heir to the honourable name of his fathers.

On the evening of this eventful day I was sitting again with my patient, who could now, however, scarcely be considered one, for the burden which had been lifted from his heart had removed his bodily sufferings. I had leisure enough now to talk every thing over with him, and there was no longer any secret between us.

Mortimer—the happy Mortimer—was in the mean time again seated with his guests at his riotous table, this time doubly intoxicated; first from the cellar of his father, and secondly from the excess of his happiness, which he believed now could not be destroyed.

For me only one thing remained to be done before I took my leave; I must arrange the plan by which Percy was to return to his father, and his father himself must place the power to carry it out in my hands. I naturally considered the accomplishment of this plan easy, when the most important event, the reconciliation, had already been effected.

" And now I can see him again," said the marquis to me; " I will see *my son* for the first time, for you assure me he has forgiven me ? "

" And *where* will you see him, my lord ? " I asked.

" *Not* here, certainly; not here ! I am no longer ill, and, therefore, no longer require a doctor near me; and besides, I do not like being in this house. To-morrow I will go to Codrington Hall. I am quite strong enough for that. In the same house will I receive him *as a father,* out of which I drove him *unlike a father;* in the same room in which I *cursed* him, will I give him *my blessing.*"

"So be it," said I; "that will be the best; he will believe that he comes for the first time to Codrington Hall; he sees his father for the first time, whom he has not yet learned to know."

"But when will you bring him to me?" asked Lord Seymour, with a countenance which somewhat astonished me, it bore such an expression of fear and mystery.

"When you command it, my lord," I replied. "You give me your orders in writing, and with those it will be an easy matter to restore him to liberty."

The old man seemed occupied with some painful thoughts; he shook his head, and looking anxiously, he said in a low voice,—

"No sir! I cannot do that!"

"What, my lord, you cannot do that?"

"Be quiet—quiet—Mortimer might be near us; do you forget that I have still another son? and that son is Mortimer!"

"What? and ——" I stammered, for I already guessed the miserable reason of his newly awakened fear.

"No, no! dare I venture to do *that,* when Mortimer

is near me. If he found it out?—if, later, he found it out in any way that I—I—myself had ordered his release, without his consent?—in writing?—no, no, I *dare* not do it."

I looked at the old man, racked by this new torture, with the greatest surprise and agitation; this refusal I had not in the least expected.

"Why can you not do it?" I asked; "are you not your own master? Are you not the Marquis of Seymour, and have you not yourself —— "

"Ah, sir! you forget what Mortimer is. He would murder me—in the night—in my sleep. And as I was before afraid of Percy's face, *his* face would destroy me."

"Ha!" cried I; "is it then from fear of Mortimer?"

"It is. Yes, it is!"

"But," I continued, "if he came of his own accord, what then? If he escaped, and came to you—threw himself at your feet, on your heart, would you still then be afraid?"

"No, no; if he came of his own accord, that would be quite a different thing; and if he were only once here, Percy would protect me against Mortimer. But where should I get the courage to conceal the truth if he asked me, 'Did you call him here?' Ah! I feel so weak when Mortimer only looks at me!"

"Well, then he shall come himself, of his own accord; and, my lord, may I come with him?"

THE MADMAN OF ST. JAMES'. 247

"Oh, sir! come with him—come with him. I have to thank you—then for my thanks, but not before; you must complete your noble work, and I —I must first see him—have him—hold him. And first he must save me, save me from Mortimer; then, for my thanks—my fatherly thanks!"

And so it was determined.

The next morning I stood before the Marquis of Seymour, dressed for my journey, and ready to set out. Lord Mortimer was present.

"I am going," said I; "your lordship no longer requires me."

"And I am going too," said Lord Seymour; "I am going to Codrington Hall. Will you go with me, Mortimer?"

"I will go on before," he answered thoughtfully; "I shall have to go rather out of the way; there is some business I have to attend to myself first; but after all, perhaps I shall be there before you: and so I wish you good-bye till then!"

And with this he turned to go away, for he had already taken leave of me.

"Mortimer!" cried the aged father.

"Well! what do you want?"

"You are going. You may never see your father again—there—my hand ——"

Mortimer coldly took his father's hand—that poor hand! it could now give him nothing more!

"You used to kiss this hand formerly."

248   THE MADMAN OF ST. JAMES'.

"I kiss it now," said Mortimer, bending quickly over it. "Good-bye!"

And with his usual loud and heavy step he went out.

"Go!" thought I; "go! If you arrive at Codrington Hall before him, the ghost of St. James' will receive you!"

CHAPTER XI.

TWO DOCTORS TO ONE PATIENT.

In the Marquis of Seymour's carriage I rolled towards London, and immediately drove to the residence of Sir John ——.

When I entered his room, I found him just where I had left him a few days ago, sitting at his writing table, and again he stretched out his friendly hand directly he saw me.

"Ah! little Job, come back already? Glad to see you. Did you find ground?"

"Very good ground, even anchorage, my dear sir!" I answered, "and I only threw out half my line!"

"Ha! well said! And what did you find at the bottom, eh?"

"Pearls, sir! real pearls of inestimable value."

"Ha! ha! devil of a fellow, that little Job! Better said still; and where is your secret?"

"With your permission, Sir John, I will keep that to myself for some time longer; but you shall know it at the right time, depend upon it; independently of this, it cannot remain long hid."

250   THE MADMAN OF ST. JAMES'.

"Well, then it is no longer a secret. Ha! ha! don't you see what I told you? I would not know it at first because I thought it would turn out so. Out of every ten secrets that one confides to one's dear friends one would always like to have nine of them back again—that is an old story." "Well," he continued, after a fit of coughing, turning round to me, "but you will dine with me?"

"On no account, sir," I answered, and got up from my chair, on which I had but just seated myself; for by this question I was reminded that every moment was precious.

"And why not, little Job? Business again already?"

"Yes, indeed, Sir John, and most important business, which does not permit an hour's delay."

"Ha, ha! a secret affair——?"

"It is the same, always the same, Sir John."

"Indeed. And where are you bound to now?"

"Back to St. James'."

"Back to St. James', eh? Always with lunatics: keep your own head clear, little Job; you begin too early; was already past forty when I got a taste for it. Dangerous thing that for a young man; the world becomes too soon serious for him; troubles come soon enough. Ha! but not on horseback again, eh?"

"Yes, Sir John, that is just the task I have to perform."

THE MADMAN OF ST. JAMES'. 251

"Thank you; only ridden once in my life, and even to this day feel I have had enough of it; lost the stirrups directly. Ha, ha!—puff—there I lay! Men are hard-mouthed enough for me without being bothered with horses. *Apropos* about St. James', do you know what question it was that Mr. Lorenz, the superintendent-physician, asked me?"

"No, I do not."

"Stupid idiot! Tells me a story about a man whom he has had four years under his care, and, all of a sudden, he does not know if he is mad or not—gets all at once a twinge of conscience."

"Ah!" I exclaimed, full of astonishment. "Mr. Sidney?"

"Right, right; what, do you know that too, little Job? And now, in my answer, I am to give him my opinion; as if one could do that so easily without having seen the man. Don't understand the doctor. Mad, or not mad, is a question, like 'To be, or not to be?' that is not so easily settled, eh?"

"Do not write it," I said, "I will give it verbally."

"Well said, little Job; very sharply remarked; but will it even then be an answer, eh?"

"You need not give me any answer at all, Sir John. Let me answer for you."

Sir John regarded me with a sharp inquiring look.

"Well, sir," said he seriously, "but you see that is my affair."

"And it shall remain your affair, my dear sir; I

will give no answer which can either injure you or your reputation."

"Ha, mysteries with me too? That goes a little too far. Who is this Mr. Sidney?"

"Know then, sir," said I, "that it was on Mr. Sidney's account that I wrote to you from St. James', and begged you to call me here; it is in Mr. Sidney's cause that I have been at Lord Seymour's. Yes, and lastly it is on Mr. Sidney's account that I am now returning to St. James', and returning on horseback."

"Ah! is that it? Well, well, really there is something in it, then."

"Certainly! And again, it was Mr. Sidney's secret that I wanted to tell you, and you would not hear it; and which now, after mature reflection, I wish to keep to myself a little while longer. You will pardon this selfishness, I hope; but I should like to keep for myself the glory and credit of having unravelled alone the mystery of his fate."

"Yes, indeed, yes; I will forgive you, and am quite satisfied about it—don't excite yourself. Have you had any luncheon?"

"Yes, Sir John, at Lord Seymour's."

"But not with me!" And he rang the bell, so I was obliged to lunch, as I could not dine, with him.

"And with respect to Mr. Lorenz," he resumed, as I was preparing to take my leave, "shall I not

THE MADMAN OF ST. JAMES'. 253

hear from you what message you are going to give him from me?"

"Yes, sir, certainly you shall hear from me;" I answered, smiling; "and you shall hear at once. I shall give an opinion which does *not* come from you, but which shall appear to come from you, and Mr. Lorenz shall come to the conclusion that it is the only correct opinion, although you have at this moment no idea of your own opinion yourself."

"Ha! ha! there we have it; that is past my poor comprehension, little Job; that is droll enough—ha! ha! Well, I am ready; go on; have you had enough?"

"Enough? Yes, for three days, sir! And now farewell."

"Good-bye, dealer in mystery! Good-bye, little Job; good luck to your journey." And he shook me heartily by the hand.

I now went quickly back to my hotel. Bob, who had been longing for my return, was almost beside himself with joy at seeing me again. My first question was, "How are the horses, Bob?"

"All right, sir; Bravour is quite unmanageable, and the little one, too. Are we soon going on again?"

"Going on? Directly, Bob; get ready, and when you have got all in order, let me know."

254   THE MADMAN OF ST. JAMES'.

Bob went out, and sent me the waiter with the
bill. As soon as everything was settled, I began to
think if it were not time to let *somebody* receive
some tidings of me; but I determined to wait a little
longer, until I had visited the late Sir William
Graham's estate, which had been sold, and where I
hoped to get some intelligence of the present place of
residence of his brother, Sir Robert Graham; particularly as I had reason to fear that Mortimer might
be before me, or might even commit some act of
violence which might render all my exertions useless.
Whatever intelligence I might obtain, I would at
once communicate it to Percy and Phillips, and
prepare them both for my return, and appoint the
latter to proceed directly to St. James.'

When Bob led out the horses into the courtyard
and I mounted, my mind became agitated in a most
extraordinary manner. Without thinking of anything
in particular, I suddenly felt, I might say, a perfect
flush of joy, which for the moment filled my whole
heart, and drew me away, as it were, from the present.
Was this sudden feeling of joy, which vanished as
quickly as it came, the result of what I had already
accomplished? or was it a foreboding, rising from
the depths of my own soul, of that which was soon
going to befall me? I regarded, however, this extraordinary emotion as a favourable omen; but decipher
it I could *not*. For who can explain the strong
feelings which sometimes affect us? Who has pene-

trated into the inner, ever-living source of our mental
being—into that dark mysterious chamber where
thoughts are generated, where feeling is created, and
where the Godlike principle within us has established
its powerful throne during the short period of our
life and action?

We soon left London far behind us again. It
would be impossible, even if I wished it, to tax the
indulgence of the reader so heavily as to place before
him the long unconnected train of thoughts which
filled my mind on the road I was then travelling
with Bob. I myself was hardly master of them;
they carried me away with them; they sported
with me, and I bore it awhile quietly, even submis-
sively.

This kind of thing does happen to us sometimes;
more particularly if, as had just occurred to me,
an undertaking has not been accomplished by ourselves, but we owe its success to fate, or to a higher
and more enlightened power; and that these had
now worked in the result of my enterprise I dared
not doubt; and even now, when years have gone by,
and I am beyond the turmoil of its influence, I cannot
doubt it still.

Had not everything until now happened in a
different manner to that in which I had determined
to conduct it? Had I really been an active agent,
as I wished to be? No, certainly not; I had been,
on the contrary, passive. I found everything in

order, prepared for action. Every one in my place would have done the same, or rather have been quite unable to act otherwise. What I had to do was placed in my hands, in the strictest meaning of the word; as I found it, so I was obliged to accept it, whether I liked it or not.

Certainly I had learned long since, from experience, that everything which happens either to us, through us, or around us, never happens in the way in which we have thought of it, or pictured it to ourselves; and that, if we do at last reach the point at which we have aimed, we almost always attain it in quite another way than we expected or intended.

Until now it had happened thus with me. One object at least I had attained—Percy had been restored to his own. His father had at last acknowledged him. Certainly much still remained to be done, to be obtained, to be surmounted. The waves of the sea of life were not yet calmed after the great storm which had overtaken him—they still rose towering over him. The hurricane itself appeared to have been hushed: still one dark, stormy cloud was visible in the horizon of his troubled life. Like a dark, threatening spirit stood Mortimer between him and his soul's peace! That I knew well enough; but for the exorcism of this fearful spirit I relied on the powerful hand of Him who is able to still the tempest and scatter the stormy clouds. My mind, therefore, became more tranquil, I breathed more freely, and with resignation and trust I looked forward hopefully for peace and happiness.

Ah! I should perhaps have felt quite easy if I had been able to obtain some more certain information respecting Ellinor and her father. All my endeavours to discover her had until now been in vain; all the accounts I had gathered relative to her were insufficient; one only contradicted the other.

Where was she?—And Phillips? he, too, was silent? Had he been more fortunate than I had? Until now I had heard nothing of him. The places at which I might have heard some news of him I had visited and left long ago;—no trace of him anywhere. I felt sure that he was still unwearied in his exertions, but I heard no account of them.

And now Sir William Graham was dead!—he, the only one on whom I had built my hopes, and on whom I might have depended for assistance and advice in all my exertions; he, who seemed to hold Percy's fate in his hands! Poor Ellinor! still no trace of her! Nothing but the recollection of troubled years long gone by occurred to me. Her image was ever before me, and in following every trace I could find with all the eagerness of an impetuous mind, sometimes I thought some sympathy must exist between her fate and Percy, and that this power would lead her to me. But no! nothing came of it; and I became depressed and discouraged, and discontented with myself, even

258   THE MADMAN OF ST. JAMES'.

enough to doubt my own ability. Sometimes I
thought that had I taken more pains, been quicker and
more determined; had I been any one else than my
own self, perhaps long since I might have found her,
and then with a lighter heart I should have been
able to return to Percy.

But these hypochondriacal lamentations—I must
call them so myself—did no good. I was forced to
resign myself to what could not be altered, and I did
resign myself, and hoped on—hoped on—but every
passing hour with weakened confidence, and with
despairing resignation at my protracted anxiety.

From all these feelings and thoughts I was aroused
by my young companion, who asked me which was
to be our next place of destination.

"I really cannot tell you, Bob, with any certainty,"
I answered; "we are now on the way to St. James',
and I have the intention of joining your father; but
first we must go rather out of our way to visit the
estate which formerly belonged to the late Sir
William Graham, to make some inquiries there
respecting his brother, the clergyman, and his
daughter."

"That is all right," said the boy; "I don't
mind where I go—the farther the better. Did you
give my compliments to the 'black man' for me,
sir?"

"Yes, Bob," answered I, smiling; "that I did in
my own way; but I did not find him quite so black

THE MADMAN OF ST. JAMES'. 259

as you pictured him to be. Lord Mortimer is much blacker."

Bob looked at me sorrowfully and answered,—

"I thought so too; an old man is never so bad as a young one, for he must begin to think of death."

So much truth lay in this *naïve* remark of the boy, and he uttered it in such a touching and simple manner, and it suited so well with the present circumstances, that I involuntarily lost myself in thinking over his words, the full weight of which he himself certainly did not know.

It was already near twelve o'clock when we drew near the castle of Lord Seymour. I could see that building lying to my left in which I had gone through my last adventure, and the way in which I had successfully accomplished it inspired me with fresh courage and energy, and more hope and trust for the future.

"Let us ride on quickly, Bob," said I; "I have made particular inquiries, and we have still twenty miles to ride from here to Graham House, and it is there I think of stopping for the night."

Without speaking much, we rode on several miles further; then we fed and watered our horses, and the evening began to close in with its pale light, as we came into the neighbourhood which formerly appeared to me so bright with hope, and now seemed to offer none.

It was a quiet and refreshing place to look upon.

s 2

Fruitful and well-cultivated fields, here and there covered with stubble; shady woods, verdant lawns, which are so common and so beautiful in England; all these lay spread before us far and wide; and at last, through an opening in the wood through which we were riding, we saw the long wished-for Graham House not far from us.

As we approached, we at once remarked that it must have changed owners. The house, although an elegant one, was still only a building of one story; at present very little could be said of the garden and grounds which surrounded it, for bricklayers and carpenters, with their materials and tools, had taken up all the spare room. The roof was off; for the new proprietor was about to add another floor, besides two wings to the building; and temporary wooden sheds had been erected in the grounds, in which those workmen lived who came from a distance. Now, as the evening drew in (for the bell had long since sounded which ended their labour until the following day), everything was unusually still; neither the sound of the axe nor the hammer could be heard; only here and there could be seen a tired workman lying on the grass near his shed, eating his supper, or smoking his pipe.

On riding round the place, it soon occurred to me that in that dilapidated house no one could be living, and I therefore was obliged to address myself to one

THE MADMAN OF ST. JAMES'. 261

of these workmen for the information I was so anxious to obtain.

Just as I was going towards one of the sheds, a man with a stick in his hand, and smoking a pipe, came up to me, and asked me what I wanted.

" Good evening, my friend ! Is there no person, no overseer or master-builder here, with whom I could speak a few words ? "

" No, sir ; the architect is not here at present ; for he only comes here every two or three days. This afternoon I have been acting for him."

" Ah ! I am glad to hear it. To whom does this house belong ? "

" Formerly it belonged to Sir William Graham ; now it is the property of Sir Charles Osbeck."

" How long is it since Sir William died ? "

" About two months, sir."

" Did he live in this large house alone ? "

" No, sir, no ; his family were with him ; a younger brother—his heir, I believe—and his daughter, if I am not mistaken."

" And when did the heir sell the house ? "

" That, sir, I do not know."

" How long is it since they left ? "

" Well, about eight weeks—at least, I should think about eight weeks."

Eight weeks ago Ellinor had been with her father at Dunsdale. It became now clearer to me that they had undertaken this journey in order to apprise Percy of their change of residence.

"Ah! that letter — that unfortunate letter!" thought I; and I felt, and I suppose *looked* so sorry about it, that I quite forgot the man gazing sympathizingly upon me, as well as everything else.

"And is there nobody here," I asked, "who could tell me where Sir Robert Graham and his daughter are gone?"

"Very sorry, sir—there is nobody here; to-day only an old servant of the family went by postchaise to London."

"By postchaise to London?" I quickly repeated, "and did he leave no message behind?"

"Nothing at all, sir. But in a week, I believe, he will be back again."

"In a week; that is something at least. But do you happen to know to whom he is gone in London?"

"Indeed, sir, I do not. London is a large place."

"It is, it is, unfortunately. Is there any place in the neighbourhood where I could remain with my horses for the night?"

"Yes, sir, about a mile and a half farther on there is an inn; a small one it is, but pretty good. It is built on Sir William's property—Sir Charles Osbeck's I mean,—and yonder is the road to it."

"Thank you, my friend. Good night then."

"Good night, sir. Make haste and get there, for

your horses seem tired, particularly that little one; he is quite covered with foam. Good night, sir."

I was already riding on, after having called Bob to me, who was still lingering behind, looking back at the man.

"What do you keep looking back for, Bob?" I asked. "Come, it is getting dark as well as late."

"I don't know, sir; but that man is staring at you so. Ha, he is beckoning; shall I ride back?"

I looked round, and certainly the man was beckoning with his stick; and now we could hear him call out too—

"I beg your pardon, sir," said he, as he drew near, and took off his hat—"I beg your pardon for detaining you any longer; but I should like to be allowed to ask you a question."

"Well, go on."

"Are you known, perhaps, in the county of Dunsdale?"

I looked at him with surprise, and pulled back my horse, which was eager to be going.

"How did you hit upon that, friend? I am very well known there."

"Well, I am glad of it; for it will be all right then. I only just recognised you by your horse, from the man's hurried description."

"Ha! what man?"

"Yes, sir; about the middle of the day a man came here on horseback from Dunsdale Castle. He was in livery, black and silver; and he said he had got a letter for some gentleman who had been at Dunsdale, and who would be found here at Sir William Graham's. He had found out the address in London."

He had not half finished before I had leaped from my horse, and gone close up to him.

"For Heaven's sake, tell me where is the man and the letter!"

"Yes, sir; he is gone. He just arrived as Mr. Cocksburn was getting into his postchaise, and I only happened to hear him speak a few words with him."

"And do you know nothing more of him—which way he went, or what Mr. Cocksburn said to him?"

"He was very sorry, sir, that he could not stop longer to hear what he had to say; but he told him that Sir Robert Graham had sold the property, and had gone away."

"And did he not say where he had gone?"

"I don't think he told him that, sir; for there have been so many inquiries made here about Sir Robert, and I believe he was forbidden to tell anybody about where he is now living."

All now became clearer to me; I thought immediately of Mortimer and his spies, and could well imagine why Graham had sold this estate, which bordered so closely on the property of the Marquis of Seymour.

"But it is still possible," said I, "that this messenger from Dunsdale Castle may have found it out. Where was he going?"

"Yonder, sir, towards the inn which I named to you; he wanted to bait his horse there, and he galloped on bravely. It was a noble animal he had, and you will not be able to overtake him; but *that* yonder is the road."

"Well, then, once more, good night, and thank you kindly, my friend; it is time that I go after him." And throwing myself on my horse, and urging on Bob, I trotted quickly on the way he pointed out.

"The horses! oh, the horses!" sighed Bob.

"Never mind the horses—never mind them; now is the time. And if yours should die, I will buy you another; Bravour will be able to stand it."

We had now a hope, a faint one it is true, but still sufficient to give me fresh courage, and to throw all my moral strength and activity into a new channel. How relieved I felt! how light, how hopeful! All heaviness had vanished from my mind; I was as fresh as if I had only begun my journey yesterday, and as if to-day I should attain my object.

Although I could not overtake the messenger to-day, for he was too far on before me, yet still I could follow his traces; and if I always rested at night at the places where he had stopped and rested, surely I must find him at last. For the present I thought of nothing else; but gradually it became darker and darker. Our horses trotted on bravely, although the pony sometimes lagged behind, and was covered with white foam.

"Well, sir," suddenly gasped out Bob, "I really don't know why we are in such a hurry; it won't be daylight again to-day, and if we are not to go on farther than that inn, we might just as well walk there; my poor little pony has not got a dry hair, and is already beginning to stumble."

I immediately pulled up, and said,—

"You are more reasonable than I am, Bob; but do not be vexed; if ever I see a glimmer of light before me, I can find no rest until I have got the light itself."

"Where is there a glimmer of light?" asked Bob, "I do not see any."

"I am speaking figuratively, Bob. By light I mean hope; by means of that letter the messenger is bringing to me I have the hope of finding Sir Robert Graham, or at least of finding out where he is living."

"Then, sir, you have now a better prospect of seeing your wish fulfilled, you think?"

"Better than ever; and that is why I am hurrying on. A little luck, Bob, and we have reached the goal."

"Ha! ha!" laughed the boy; "as my father says, a drachm of luck is worth more than an ounce of sense."

"Not always, my boy; opportunities will still

THE MADMAN OF ST. JAMES'. 267

come to prove to you that nothing can replace sense. But see! there, I believe, is the inn!"

And so it was; close before us, just where the high road crossed the wood-path, it stood, half hidden by a high hawthorn hedge.

On dismounting, I desired Bob to see that the horses had double feed, and the softest straw; for no one could know what might be required of them the day following.

In answer to my first inquiry I ascertained from the landlord that the man I was following had really been there, but—had gone away some hours before. Fortunately he had named a place about eight miles distant, where he said he should stop for the night, and his destination the next day was a village, C——, about twenty-eight miles beyond that.

This information was of the highest importance to me; of course his road was my road, but still I had not yet decided if I should not ride on the next morning quite early before daybreak, and thus find him at his night's lodging; or, if I should allow the horses a few hours' more rest, and, performing a longer journey than he would, meet him in the evening at the village of C——. After some reflection, I preferred the latter; first because the horses must be spared, and besides, it was possible this man might also begin his journey before daybreak, and if he did, notwithstanding all my haste, he would still be in advance of me.

Had I, however, found at the inn a carriage or a fresh horse, I might have gone on immediately, even in the night, to try and overtake him, although I knew nothing of the road, and the least mistake might have taken me out of the right way; but as there was neither carriage nor horse to be had, I had to wait quietly for the next day, and patiently abide by the resolution I had formed.

And this resolution was the best, and justified by the result; for when we arrived the next morning at the place where the messenger had spent the night, we heard he had started on his way very early, so that under any circumstances we should not have found him.

Our journey this day led us through one of the most beautiful parts of England; at least, one in which cultivation had done its noblest work. In every direction could be seen gentle slopes, and the trees and the fields were clothed with a most beautiful green. Here, in quick succession, we passed picturesque country seats of the richest nobles of the land, parks filled with deer, garden grounds laid out in the best taste, with winding streams and fountains, all in the most perfect order and beauty.

Bob was delighted; never had he pictured to himself the wide world so beautiful; and more than once I was obliged to hurry him away from places which he considered unequalled in beauty; and continually was he exclaiming, "Ah! how splendid! Oh! how beautiful is this!"

THE MADMAN OF ST. JAMES'. 269

" By and by you will be able to admire this more at your leisure, my boy," said I, " but to-day we must hurry on, for every moment of delay appears to me to be a crime "

And so it did : the farther I went, the longer my journey lasted, the more I longed to hurry on; and had not Bob and his wicked nag been with me, I might have tried to perform a double journey that day, for Bravour did not seem to know what fatigue was; no moisture disfigured his glossy skin, and he was just as fiery and spirited, and his step in the evening was just as light and sure, as when we started in the morning.

At last we arrived at the already mentioned village of C——, and at the only inn there we heard that, a few hours before we arrived, a horseman had taken some refreshment, after which in haste he had taken another horse, and had gone on. This was certainly *not* what I had anticipated; and, what was worse, nobody could tell me his destination. The horse he had ridden ·on his wearisome and hurried journey he had left behind, and hired another from the innkeeper.

I immediately went to the stable, and recognised in the large bay blood horse there one of the handsomest horses belonging to the Viscount of Dunsdale, which I had already seen and admired at the castle. The noble animal was not overworked, but had gone lame from a little stone having got in between the iron shoe and the hoof. The messenger had said that he would return in a few days and take him away, and bring back to the owner the horse he had hired. His place of destination could not therefore be very far distant, and this reflection made my mind easy in some degree.

After we had heard an accurate description of the road which the swift rider before us had taken, we again resumed our journey quite early the next morning. The road was more than usually sandy, and very tiring for the horses; we therefore proceeded somewhat slowly. But we could see in the sand traces of the rider who had preceded us, and followed them; for this to us was a great advantage. Suddenly, however, the sandy road came to an end, and we came on to a sort of common, where to follow the traces of the horse was no longer possible, but still we hopefully rode on.

It might have been about eleven o'clock in the morning, when suddenly the road before us branched off to the right and left, and we halted for a while, doubtful which of these two roads we should take.

"This is the worst thing that could happen to us, Bob," said I; "and I have been afraid for some time it would come to this! Now it is difficult to know what to do; for while we ride to the right, perhaps our messenger with the letter may have gone to the left, and if we but miss him for one day we shall never get hold of him again."

THE MADMAN OF ST. JAMES'. 271

We both looked attentively around us. There were the wide and large stubble-fields, but no signs of a human habitation, and no living creature of whom we could ask a question.

At last the simple idea occurred to Bob that we should leave the choice of a road to our horses, and abide by it as if it were the decision of an oracle.

"You wanted me to believe that sense was worth more than luck, sir," said he; "very well; but I still, however, hold to the luck; so let us try it now."

"I quite agree to it," I replied; "we will ride back a little way, and then let our horses run their own road, and whichever they choose, that road we will take too. Now for it."

We rode back, then gave our horses the reins, and set off quickly for the starting place; Bob rode on the left, I on the right.

A curious circumstance now took place—which least of all we had expected—for Bob's little pony took the road to the left, but Bravour took the road to the right; consequently, we were immediately separated, and soon lost sight of each other, owing to the green hedge which for some distance ran between the two roads. We quickly pulled up, stopped the horses, and, laughing heartily, returned again to the place from which we had started.

"Now which is the clever horse, and which is the lucky one?" called out Bob; "that, sir, you will find it difficult to decide."

272 THE MADMAN OF ST. JAMES'.

"We will not abuse fate, and still less will we separate, Bob. Let us, therefore, return again, and at a walking pace try the same experiment, and the result shall decide it."

So we rode back, and, with a loose bridle, let our horses walk. This time they remained close beside each other, and both took the road to the right, which Bravour had chosen with me at first. Bob was again going to dispute about it, when I cut him short with the simple remark,—

"Bravour has chosen for the second time the same road, and Puck the pony has followed him ;—it is, therefore, settled, Bob ; let us ride this way."

And we slowly rode down the road to the right. But twelve o'clock came, and still we could discover no traces of what we were looking for. We certainly met some. country people, but not one of them had seen the rider we followed ; if they had, his dress alone would have caused him to be remarked. During the hottest part of the day we rested and refreshed ourselves and the horses in a little farmhouse, the master of which assured us that no rider had passed their door for four-and-twenty hours. This certainly was not much consolation, and I gradually began to feel some uneasiness about the right choice of our road.

But we again mounted and resumed our journey, and my young companion smiled roguishly at me two or three times, as if he would thereby give me to understand that we were on the wrong track, and that the path which he had chosen, had been the right one. He did not, however, say anything about it, as he observed that I perseveringly adhered to my resolution, and continued steadily on my way. And indeed there was something within me—shall I call it obstinacy or caprice?—which involuntarily drew me onwards; an unknown impelling power, which seemed to bid me go on with confidence and have no more misgivings. We rode side by side in silence, my looks, following the dictates of my heart, glancing with a certain degree of anxiety upon everything we passed, noticing every path, and bestowing the greatest attention on every object.

It was now afternoon. This also went by, and the evening drew near. But, ah, what an evening! A gentle breeze, hardly to be felt, had long since carried away on its cooling wings the sultry heat of the day, and the air was again so mild, one could hardly remark its tender breathings, and withal so pure and fragrant, that I should have liked to have drawn a thousand breaths in one minute to have more completely inhaled its fresh, living perfume.

But the short interval which precedes twilight also went by, and the evening with its full splendour spread its solemn shades over the lovely spot, accompanied by its constant attendant, that holy calm, which purifies the hearts of men, and is the forerunner of the still more tranquil, but less friendly, night.

VOL. II.

274 THE MADMAN OF ST. JAMES'.

The light was fading gradually away, and distant objects began to mix one with another; then arose a faint mist, more to be felt than seen, which, like a half-transparent cloud, settled upon the wide fields, and covered hedge and valley with its airy, waving garment; and withal it was so exquisitely cool, so refreshing, so enchanting in this balmy evening air, that I stopped my horse sometimes for the purpose of contemplating the lovely scene before me.

I could not have imagined that in such a tranquil atmosphere anything so perfectly fascinating could exist, if I had not felt it myself at this moment; for never until now had I enjoyed such a beautiful evening—no, not even in warmer climates. I moved as if in a new and more purified element; a spiritual presence seemed to hover around me of loving hearts hushed into holy repose.

But perhaps my heart was disposed at this moment to receive such charming impressions. I was on my way now towards one for whom I had long searched in vain, and who was very dear to me, although I had never seen her. Ah, this difficult and vain search made me sorrowful, while it excited me to redoubled efforts to find her at last.

The sky above us was as clear and pure as a transparent lake, and only on the extreme point of the horizon gleamed a half-circle of pale red. Yonder was the sun sinking into the Atlantic Ocean.

Between us and that pale red horizon, a silvery

light seemed to shine over the green meadows, and, as if in play, to conceal itself, here behind a hill, there behind a bush, until, closely approaching us, it softly and gradually, as it had come, lost itself again in flickering windings, just as if it could not without great effort tear itself away, and depart from this enchanting spot.

The whole foreground was a green wide space, covered here and there with groups of trees. To the right and left, at equal distances from each other, gigantic haystacks had been erected, and they looked like watchmen in the quiet valley, to the fertility of which they owed their growth, and filled the air with their fragrance.

Moving about among them was a large herd of cattle and bleating sheep, and the tinkling of their bells often reached us from a distance; but no dust rose above or behind them as they passed over the green sward. To the left, in one of the deepest parts of the valley, shaded by lime-trees, stood a solitary out-building, the night-shelter of the returning herd; and before it was a house, larger perhaps than it appeared to be at a distance. Its red-tiled roof rose invitingly above the lime-trees, and before the door, like sentinels, stood two enormous poplars.

But even brighter in colour than the green turf under our feet, shone forth the green window-shutters and the glittering windows which, bathed in a fiery

purple light, seemed as if they had been breathed upon
by the setting sun, as though, in the sorrow of parting, it
had bestowed on them its brightest rays.   The whole
was enclosed by iron railings, and lay there like a
jewel in its setting.

To the right of us rose a hill, even higher than the
one upon which we stood, and separated from it by a
silvery stream, over which was thrown a small bridge ;
a similar bridge also connected the out-building with
the largest of the two hills.

Such was the scene on which we gazed in silence ;
and I have described it the more minutely, as a twofold remembrance will bind me to it for ever ; for,
not only did circumstances take place here,—circumstances which I have yet to relate,—but the very sight
of it also called forth in me the most peaceful,
sacred, and yet at the same time the most sorrowful
recollections of my youth.

At first sight I was struck with the resemblance
of this lovely spot,—with the exception of some
trifling details,—to one of the most frequented and
favourite places in my own country ; a spot which
had seen my growth from boy to man, and which
was for ever engraven on my memory.   Ah ! the
first joyful, glowing feelings of youth were connected
with it; of youth which is the only thing in our
mortal life which, when once past, is gone for ever,
and which nothing which the world possesses—wealth,
beauty, or power—can ever restore.   And this lovely

THE MADMAN OF ST. JAMES'. 277

spot, perfumed by the fragrant breath of this balmy
evening, recalled to my memory that time, and the
places where I had spent those hours of youth and
joy; and suddenly I felt such an inexpressible, half-
melancholy longing for my childhood's home, that,
giving myself up to my own thoughts, I gradually
became more and more unmindful of the present,
and the past with all its joys and sorrows took full
possession of my heart. Ah! and that past exercises
such sweet influence over us and in us, that I could
envy that being who can shed a warm tear
over it.

My searching eyes glanced over the space before
us, and remained fixed on the quiet house on the hill
above; a light smoke like a cloud issued from one of
the chimneys.

"If you who dwell there are only as peaceful as
the breeze which plays around you, and as friendly as
the spot you inhabit," thought I to myself, "then,
indeed, it must be a delight to know you;" and
at once I determined to claim the hospitality of
the inhabitants. I felt now as if I *must* pass its
inviting threshold; an irresistible power seemed to
draw me towards that house.

"But no," I thought again; "perhaps some rich
squire, without wife or child, is living there; and
what would he care for you, a stranger? You must
go on farther, and try to reach some humbler dwelling; for it would pain you to see yourself disap-

278   THE MADMAN OF ST. JAMES'.

pointed in your imaginings, and to find the inhabitants of that quiet house not corresponding with your
wishes!"   And I was just going to act on these
thoughts and turn away, when an exclamation from
Bob drew my attention for a moment to another
object.

"Look, sir!" cried he; "there!—on the top of
the hill yonder, is a man on horseback, standing still,
and, like us, looking about him."

"Where?—there? Yes, indeed; so it is, a man on
horseback."

But, important as this discovery was for me, yet
I could scarcely rouse myself from the profound
reflections into which I had fallen.

"Ride up to him, Bob," I said, softly; "from
here one can hardly see what he looks like. Ride up,
and see who he is."

Bob rode cautiously down the slippery declivity, and
I was again alone. Once more I hurriedly looked at
the surrounding country—the house, the poplars, the
horizon, and thought of my own home far away—and
then slowly rode on to meet Bob, who, in the mean
time had got up to the rider, exchanged a few words
with him, and was now returning to me just as com-
posedly as he had ridden away.

"It is nothing," thought I; "otherwise Bob would
certainly ride back quicker; it is nothing, after all."

"It was not he, sir," said Bob, when he got near
to me; "it is a doctor from the next town, who has

THE MADMAN OF ST. JAMES'. 279

been sent for to see somebody who is ill there." And with that he pointed to the quiet house which lay to our left.

"A doctor, too!" thought I, "who has been called in to somebody who is ill. So, somebody is ill under that peaceful roof! Ah! I also am seeking one who is suffering—one whose heart is suffering—to whom I am the bearer of a precious and healing balm." And we rode up in silence towards the little bridge, which we had to cross in order to get to the other side of the stream.

But the horseman was also from the other side wending his way towards the bridge; therefore, in the middle of it we met. I just looked at him, and then turning to the left, in order to avoid an opening at the side, I quietly pursued my way.

But Bob happened to remain behind. He had got off his horse in order to buckle the girth of his saddle tighter, for it had slipped.

I rode on slowly, and gradually approached the house, which looked larger and handsomer the nearer I came. I once more stood still, and involuntarily looked at it. I could now distinctly see a man standing within the iron railings, but, on account of the increased darkness, I could not clearly distinguish his face. Then it seemed to me as if I saw something dark move at the feet of this man; I looked more attentively, a moment passed, and then I perceived a large, very large, black dog, who, stretching out his neck, and with his long tail trailing on the ground, came from behind the railings, first advancing slowly, almost creeping, then quicker and quicker, until at last, with tremendous bounds, it sprang towards me.

I stopped Bravour; I heard a loud repeated whistle, but the dog did not heed it.

I seized my large riding-whip, for the dog was already quite close to me, and he seemed to fix his eye on me. I could see its immense head, and the thick hair, which bristled like a lion's mane round its neck, its broad chest, and its large sharp white teeth; but notwithstanding its savage appearance, it did not seem to have any unfriendly intentions, but kept quite quiet until he was close at my side; when he suddenly uttered a loud piercing howl, rose up on his hind-legs, and placed his fore-paws on the neck of my horse, and then again behind me on its back, snuffing, smelling, and then finally breaking out into a still louder and more joyful yell than before, and in the greatest delight leaping round me.

Bravour stood at first quite quiet, attentively observing the dog; at the first howl, he pricked up his ears, and then at last, breaking out into an unusually loud neigh, he bent his arched neck towards the dog, which so caressingly jumped up to him.

As if fascinated, I silently observed this scene.

THE MADMAN OF ST. JAMES'. 281

At this moment Bob came riding up. I looked round towards him in astonishment.

"Ha! Othello, Othello! Why, that is Othello!" I heard him exclaim; and then, like scales falling from my eyes and heart, I had forgotten all my dreams; the country, the house, my home far away, all were forgotten; and with almost a feeling of pain in my heart, I sprang from my horse. Bob did the same, and went towards the dog. But the animal, as if mad with joy, sprang, barking, towards the railings, and now the man I had seen behind them came forward. All was dark, quite dark before my eyes, but in my mind it was as clear as morning light; for I saw—I saw with my mind's eyes—Mr. Graham standing before me.

Suddenly my heart seemed to stop beating; a dreadful fear seized me, and then immediately afterwards came a feeling of inexpressible relief. At a sign from me, Bob, who was on the point of speaking, quietly stepped back, took hold of the bridles of the horses, and led them a few steps from us.

One instant more, and I had collected myself. I knew now what to do, what to say, and I set to work immediately.

" Sir !" said I, going up to the reverend gentleman, whose face I could scarcely see, " are you expecting a doctor ?"

"Ah ! is it you, sir?" he asked, quickly, offering me

his hand; "I have waited for you a long time. Oh! my child, my child;—down, Othello. Be quiet! What is the matter? Go away!" and the dog went to the place where Bob stood with the horses. I was just going to look that way, when another scene for the moment occupied my whole attention. The other horseman in the mean time had also came up, and bowing politely to us, introduced himself as the doctor who had been sent for to attend the sick lady.

"Excuse me, sir," said I, in a somewhat agitated voice to Sir Robert Graham,—for it was indeed he, —"I have a few words to speak with this gentleman. Pray, will you be so kind as to enter the house first? —I will follow you immediately."

Sir Robert looked a little surprised at the two doctors arriving at the same time, but he bowed, raised for a moment the small black velvet cap which covered his head, and then withdrew.

"Sir," said I to the doctor, going close to the side of his horse, for he had not yet dismounted, "sir," said I, in the most friendly voice possible, "I have not the honour of knowing you, and I therefore must beg you will excuse a somewhat bold request. I have also been called in to this patient;—and—I should like—should like—to attend this case myself —alone!"

The doctor naturally looked at me a little sur-

THE MADMAN OF ST. JAMES'. 283

prised, but he was not angry, and merely said,—
" What, sir ? "

I repeated my request, adding, " It is extraordinary that we meet here ; but I have the most important reasons for wishing to visit this patient quite alone. Allow us to-morrow to have the honour of your visit, and, if your assistance should then be necessary, we shall be most happy to have it. I promise you a hearty welcome, and the sincere thanks of Sir Robert Graham."

" Ah ! well—you are then a doctor also ?—most likely from L——— ?   Well, well ;—but it is very singular."

" Most singular indeed, sir, I confess ; but I intreat you earnestly to accede to my request ; there is some mistake—a secret, if you like, is connected with my appearance here.   May I hope to see you again to-morrow ?"

" Ah ! I understand, sir !" said the good-natured doctor, " I understand ;—in a hurry, I suppose ; several doctors have been sent for at once, and you were here before me.   Well—it is all right—I will go—good night, sir ! good night !"

And he immediately turned his horse's head.

I should really have liked to take this good man into the room with me ;—but—ought a stranger to be present to hear what I had to say ?

" To-morrow you will come for certain ?—to dinner ?" I added ; " I beg you to do it."

284 THE MADMAN OF ST. JAMES'.

"Very well, sir, very well; I shall come!"

"I thank you, sir! to-morrow you shall hear more." And he rode away;—but I?——

I entered the house of Sir Robert Graham, formerly the clergyman of Codrington.

END OF VOL. II.

3 AU60

LONDON: J. F. HOPE, 16, GREAT MARLBOROUGH STREET.

NEW WORKS

PUBLISHED BY

J. F. HOPE,

16, GREAT MARLBOROUGH STREET, LONDON.

——o——

In 2 vols., post 8vo, price 21s.

Sheridan and his Times. By an Octogenarian who Stood by his Knee in Youth, and Sat at his Table in Manhood. [*Ready*.

"Whatever Sheridan has done, or chosen to do, has been, *par excellence*, always the best of its kind. He has written the best comedy, the best opera, the best farce (it is only too good for a farce), and the best address—the monologue on Garrick—and, to crown all, delivered the very best oration—the famous Begum speech—ever conceived or heard in this country."—*Byron*.

London : J. F. Hope, 16, Great Marlborough-street.

————

In 2 vols., post 8vo, price 21s.

Historical Recollections of the Reign of William the Fourth, including the Parliamentary Reformation of Great Britain and Ireland. By A. J. Maley.

London : J. F. Hope, 16, Great Marlborough-street.

————

In 1 vol., post 8vo, price 10s. 6d.

Frank Marland's Manuscripts ; or, Memoirs of a Modern Templar. By F. Frederick Brandt.

London : J. F. Hope, 16, Great Marlborough-street.

————

In 1 vol., post 8vo, price 10s. 6d.

Zymé ; or, How it Works. By J. S. H.

London : J. F. Hope, 16, Great Marlborough-street.

In 3 vols. post 8vo, price 31s. 6d.

"The Madman of St. James'." From the
Diary of a Physician. [*Nearly ready.*

London: J. F. Hope, 16, Great Marlborough-street.

In 1 vol., post 8vo, price 10s.

"Persuasions." By the Rev. T. Hanley
Ball, St. Andrew's Church, Holborn.

London: J. F. Hope, 16, Great Marlborough-street.

In 1 vol., demy 8vo, price 10s. 6d.

"Man:" Considered in Relation to a Present
and Future State of Being.
By the Rev. JOHN LOCKHART ROSS, M.A.,
Vicar of Avebury-cum-Winterbourne, Monkton, Wilts,
Author of "The Traces of Primitive Truth,"
"The Church and the Civil Power,"
"Letters on Secession to Rome," &c.

[*Ready.*

London: J. F. Hope, 16, Great Marlborough-street.

In 2 vols. post 8vo, price 21s.

The Old Chateau. [*Ready.*

London: J. F. Hope, 16, Great Marlborough-street.

Price 2s.

"Fur and Feathers." By F. Frederick
Brandt.

London: J. F. Hope, 16, Great Marlborough-street.

In 1 vol., post 8vo, price 10s. 6d. [*In the Press.*

A False Step in Life: a True Story.

London: J. F. Hope, 16, Great Marlborough-street.

In 1 vol., post 8vo, price 10s. 6d. Illustrated [*In the Press.*

"Experiences in Australia." By a Lady.

London: J. F. Hope, 16, Great Marlborough-street.

J. F. HOPE, GREAT MARLBOROUGH-STREET. 3

AT ALL THE LIBRARIES.

NEW WORK by C. F. HOWARD.

In 2 vols., post 8vo, price 21s.

Gilbert Midhurst, M.P. By Charles F.

Howard, Author of " Olympus," " Essays for the Age," &c.

" Gilbert Midhurst remains a remarkable book—a book replete with thought and with incentives to thought. It is the book to attract men and women of robuster intellectual frame—men and women who take life in earnest, and recognise in the social phenomena around them problems worth studying, worth struggling to solve."—*Press.*

" Gilbert Midhurst is clever."—*Athenæum.*

" A more fearless, out-spoken writer never took pen in hand. He is in earnest in his beliefs and disbeliefs—in his loves and hates—in his scorn and contempt."—*Globe.*

In 1 vol., post 8vo, price 2s.

Essays for the Age. By Chas. F. Howard,

Author of " Gilbert Midhurst, M.P."

" The author of these essays, in whom we also recognize the author of 'Olympus,' is a bold and original thinker, who has the faculty of expressing his thoughts in terse, vigorous, and sententious language. We remember well his 'Olympus'—and what a book was that! How daring and subtle in its speculation—how cutting in its satire—how withering in its scorn! The ability of the author was apparent in every page."—*Morning Post.*

London : J. F. Hope, 16, Great Marlborough-street.

In 1 vol., post 8vo, price 3s.

Olympus. By the same Author.

" It is with regret that we close the pages of this clever book. We recommend our readers strongly to peruse it for themselves. They will find brave thoughts and noble words in it."—*The Press.*

London : J. F. Hope, 16, Great Marlborough-street.

In 1 vol., post 8vo, price 8s. 6d.

Perseus and his Philosophies. By the same

Author.

" It is instructive, and, in more ways than one, original. If the ideas strike us at times as not new, it is because they find a ready echo in the heart, and all deep pondering hath this silent response within us—the strong and more familiar, the more novel and profound."—*Court Journal.*

London : J. F. Hope, 16, Great Marlborough-street.

NEW WORKS PUBLISHED BY

NEW WORK ON INDIA.
Post 8vo, price 10s. 6d.

A Gallop to the Antipodes; returning Overland
through India, &c. By John Shaw, M.D., F.G.S., F.L.S., Author of " A Tramp to the Diggings," " A Ramble through the United States," " Recollections of Travel," &c.

London: J. F. Hope, 16, Great Marlborough-street.

In I vol., post 8vo, price 6s.

London, Past, Present, and Future. By
John Ashford, Esq., Author of " Italy's Hope," &c.

London : J. F. Hope, 16, Great Marlborough-street.

In 3 vols., post 8vo, price 31s. 6d.

Blight; or, the Novel Hater. By the Author
of " Good in Everything," &c.

" There is incident enough, character enough, and clearness enough, to furnish materials for half-a-dozen modern romances. We have already said there is considerable cleverness—we may go so far as to add genius—in this work. The lady writer has stuff enough of the right sort in her to produce a novel that shall be popular and shall keep popular."—*Leader*.

" The authoress of this work is bent upon showing that there may be good even in novels. It is clever, and the interest is sustained throughout. The fidelity with which the characters are drawn is very commendable."—*Sunday Times*.

" Whatever else the critics may say of ' Blight,' they cannot say it is a dull book. The story never stagnates. ' Blight' has the recommendation of being illustrated."—*The Bookseller*.

" Blight is described as a tale of our own times, and its object is to expose the evils of mere money-making. It purports to be the work of a lady, and as such it must be regarded as a very successful production, and is in many respects superior to the previous publication of the author, ' Good in Everything.' There is an abundance of incident in the novel, and the plot is well constructed. Under these circumstances ' Blight' will obtain a considerable amount of popularity."—*Observer*.

" We hasten to add that, as regards most excellent moral intention, good purpose, exuberance of fancy in dramatic story, and bold conceptions, the authoress of ' Blight' claims attention."—*Literary Gazette*.

London: J. F. Hope, 16, Great Marlborough-street.

Royal 16mo, price 3s.

Self. By the Rev. E. Morse, A.B., Author
of " Thoughts on the Hope of Resurrection," &c.

London : J. F. Hope, 16, Great Marlborough-street.

J. F. HOPE, GREAT MARLBOROUGH-STREET. 5

In 1 vol., post 8vo, price 7s. 6d. (Now ready.)

The Privateer. By C. Stone, Esq., 77th
Regiment, Author of the "Rifle Catechism," "Aslané," &c.

"The tale is spiritedly and pleasantly narrated, and the interest never flags."—*Observer*.

London : J. F. Hope, 16, Great Marlborough-street.

Post 8vo, price 2s. (Just ready.)

The Rifle Catechism ; or, the Philosophy of
the Rifle. By Cecil Stone, Esq., 77th Regiment, Author of "The Privateer," "Aslané," &c.

London : J. F. Hope, 16, Great Marlborough-street.

In 2 vols., post 8vo, price 21s. (Ready.)

The House of Camelot. A Tale of the Olden
Time. By Miss Mary Linwood.

"'The House of Camelot' comes to us as an agreeable variation among the novels which deal with Paris and Belgrave-square. It is written with care and enthusiasm, and may be recommended to constant readers who call at the circulating library."—*Leader*.

"'The House of Camelot' is certainly the best of the novels lately published."—*Daily Telegraph*.

London : J. F. Hope, 16, Great Marlborough-street.

In 1 vol., post 8vo, 416 pp., price 10s. 6d.

The Life and Times of Dante.
By R. de Vericour, Professor of Languages and Literature in the Queen's University, Cork.

"Those who wish to obtain an accurate knowledge of the life and times of Dante we can refer to no better book than the one before us. . . . It is evidently a scholar's labour of love, and by far the best introduction in our language to Dante's works that we remember to have seen."—*Critic*.

London : J. F. Hope, 16, Great Marlborough-street.

Second Edition, Second Series, now ready, price 6s. 6d.

Brameld's Practical Sermons.

"Full of earnest thought and genial feeling."—*Athenæum*.

"A book of a thousand merits."—*Press*.

"The claims of personal religion are enforced with singular earnestness."—*John Bull*.

London : J. F. Hope, 16, Great Marlborough-street.

NEW WORKS PUBLISHED BY

Second Edition, much improved, price 6s.

Thirty-four Practical Sermons.

By G. W. Brameld, M.A. Oxon., Vicar of East Markham, late Curate of Mansfield.

"Truly spiritual."—*John Bull.*

"Brief, earnest, and forcible."—*English Churchman.*

"These discourses are truly what they are termed in the title-page, practical. Mr. Brameld does not command belief, he persuades and convinces."—*Critic.*

London: J. F. Hope, 16, Great Marlborough-street.

Just published, price 7s. 6d.

Thirty Sermons, on Jonah, Amos, and Hosea.

By the Rev. W. Drake, M.A., Lecturer of St. John Baptist Church, Coventry; Hebrew Examiner in the University of London; and late Fellow of St. John's College, Cambridge.

London: J. F. Hope, 16, Great Marlborough-street.

Just published, price 6d.

The Prophecy of Koshru, &c. Translated

by J. D., and Edited by M.D.

London: J. F. Hope, 16, Great Marlborough-street.

NEW WORK BY MRS. ROBERT CARTWRIGHT.

In 2 vols., post 8vo, price £1 1s.

The Royal Sisters; or, Pictures of a Court.

By Mrs. R. Cartwright, Author of "Lamia," "Christabelle," "Ambrose the Sculptor," &c. &c.

London: J. F. Hope, 16, Great Marlborough-street.

Post 8vo, price 2s.   (Now ready.)

Aslané. A Tale of the Massacre of the Nestorian Christians. By C. Stone, Esq., 77th Regiment.

London: J. F. Hope, 16, Great Marlborough-street.

In 1 vol., post 8vo, price 10s. 6d.

The Odd Confidant; or, "Handsome is that Handsome Does." By Dot.

"The 'Odd Confidant' is an interesting tale, with a good moral, most pleasantly and ably worked out. It shows, with considerable power, the ill effects produced on girls by the baneful system of educating them at French schools, and the unhappiness that always ensues from the practices of concealment or deceit. . . . We cannot conclude our notice better than by heartily recommending the book for the perusal of young girls just entering upon the dangerous gaieties of fashionable life."—*Court Circular.*

London: J. F. Hope, 16, Great Marlborough-street.

J. F. HOPE, GREAT MARLBOROUGH-STREET.   7

Second Edition, post 8vo, price 3s. 6d.   (Now ready.)

Preaching, Prosing, and Puseyism, with other
Peas of the Pod.   By Feltham Burghley, Author of "Sir Edwin Gilderoy," &c.

"We have much pleasure in recommending this exceedingly clever, sparkling, learned, and out-spoken *brochure* to all our readers. Whatever some may think of its sentiments, all competent and candid judges will grant its vigour, earnestness, power, and talent—a power which sometimes approaches the transcendent, and a talent which often overpasses the verge of true genius."—*Critic.*

London : J. F. Hope, 16, Great Marlborough-street.

———

In 1 vol., post 8vo, price 6s.

A Legend of the Rhone.   By M. P. B.
London : J. F. Hope, 16, Great Marlborough-street.

———

In 1 vol., post 8vo, price 10s. 6d.   (Just Published.)

Juvenile Crime : its Causes, Character, and
Cure.   By S. P. Day, Author of " Monastic Institutions," &c.

" No one can read this volume without being convinced that Mr. Day has thoroughly mastered the subject with which he deals. . . . It is an elaborate, enlightened, and temperately but forcibly written work, and does credit alike to the intelligence and to the heart of the author. . . . Mr. Day has discharged his task well, and produced a manual which ought to be placed in the hands of every statesman and philanthropist."—*Morning Post.*

" The matter brought together is ample, and lucidly arranged, and Mr. Day himself seems to have devoted no superficial study to the problem he is ambitious of solving."—*Athenæum.*

" The very latest of our statistical publications confirm his (Mr. Day's) conclusions, and teach us that the mass of crimes which now plague the community are preventible."—*Leader.*

" Mr. Day seems to have carefully studied the latest statistics of criminality, and we can honestly recommend his work to the attention of those whose interest it is that crime should decrease and morality increase—and whom does this not interest ?"—*Critic.*

" The work abounds in important facts, culled from unquestionable sources. There can be little doubt that this volume will attract the goodwill as well as the attention of the thinking community."—*Observer.*

London : J. F. Hope, 16, Great Marlborough-street.

———

Just published, Vol. I., price 7s. 6d.; Vol. II., price 10s. 6d.   Beautifully Illustrated.

History and Antiquities of Roxburghshire
and Adjacent Districts, from the most remote period to the present time.   By Alexander Jeffrey, Esq., Author of " Guide to Antiquities of the Borders," &c.

London : J. F. Hope, 16, Great Marlborough-street.

8   NEW WORKS PUBLISHED BY

Demy 8vo, price 3s.

Duty to Parents : Honour thy Father and thy Mother.   By a Clergyman of the Church of England.

"A useful companion to persons newly confirmed."—*Guardian.*

"Excellent in its purpose and contents."—*Spectator.*

"This excellent little volume may assist the parents above alluded to.   It is a well-planned, well-executed book."—*Leader.*

"This little book, placing the duty on its true Scriptural basis, would be a useful present to most young gentlemen, and even to some young ladies too."—*Churchman's Magazine.*

London : J. F. Hope, 16, Great Marlborough-street.

STARTLING NEW WORK.

Vol. I., post 8vo, price 5s.   (Second Edition, Revised.)

Holland : its Institutions, Press, Kings, and Prisons ; with an awful Exposure of Court Secrets and Intrigues.   By E. Meeter.

"The work is written in a style which stamps the author as a master of our language, and it bears upon its every page the reality of truth."

London : J. F. Hope, 16, Great Marlborough-street.

Post 8vo, price 1s. 6d.

Arnold: a Dramatic History.

By Cradock Newton.

"There is exquisite beauty in 'Arnold.'"—*Glasgow Commonwealth.*

"'Arnold' is a book of real poetry.   It is full of beauty, and will be felt to be so by all who have a lover's passion for the great and small things both of nature and of thought, and whose delight is to see them dressed in poetic fancies again and again."—*Inquirer.*

"In toiling across a wide desert of arid verse, we are too delighted to meet with the sound of a spring or the fragrance of a flower not to give it a welcome.   Of the kind have we found in 'Arnold.'   There are evident touches of poetry in it.   The stream of the verse has a gleam of gold.   The author is apparently very young, but has undoubtedly shown that he possesses the poetic temperament.   An unusually pure tone and purpose in the book augur well for the future of the writer.   The various lyrics show a sense of music in verse. The patrons of our minstrels will do well not to pass this little pamphlet by."—*Athenæum.*

London : J. F. Hope, 16, Great Marlborough-street.

Post 8vo, price 5s.

The Pirate, and other Poems.   By C. Boot.

[*Just Ready.*

London : J. F. Hope, 16, Great Marlborough-street.

J. F. HOPE, GREAT MARLBOROUGH-STREET.   9

Price 3s.   Second Edition.

The Young Lady's First French Book, with

a Vocabulary of the French and English, and the English and French, of all the words used in the Book.   By R. Aliva.

"This work is decidedly the best we have yet seen of the kind, and we observe that our opinion is backed by our numerous contemporaries."—*Courier.*

London : J. F. Hope, 16, Great Marlborough-street.

In 1 vol, post 8vo, price 10s. 6d.   (Second Edition.)

The Adventures of Mrs. Colonel Somerset in

Caffraria.   Edited by I. E. Fenton.

"Mrs. Colonel Somerset encounters more adventures than Sindbad, and receives more blessings than Hatim Tai. . . . On the score of original observations as an African traveller she might wrangle with Dr. Livingstone. . . . And in the poetry of her reminiscences might have competed with Pietro della Valle."—*Athenæum.*

"Mrs. Somerset has some startling episodes to tell, which in another place might remind us of Munchausen."—*Weekly Dispatch.*

London : J. F. Hope, 16, Great Marlborough-street.

Post 8vo, price 2s. 6d.

First Steps in British History, for the use

of Schools and Private Families.   By the late Tutor to the Earl of Glamorgan.

"The 'young nobleman' is the Earl of Glamorgan, and whoever his tutor is, we feel on the perusal of these pages, that he is a man worthy to be trusted. The leading facts of British history are thrown into the form of a narrative, so simple that a child of six years may understand it.   Taking this excellent nursery-book from beginning to end, we should say that the main facts are truthfully stated, and the great religious and constitutional principles guarded with a vigilance that would have done credit to the authors of many more pretentious books."—*Christian Times.*

"A concise and well-written summary of the history of England, from the invasion of Julius Cæsar to our own times.   The language is simple, and, as the title premises, adapted to the comprehension of very young children ; and the author, not satisfied himself with the bare recital of historical events, seizes every opportunity of inculcating good principles by pointing out those actions worthy of admiration and imitation, and those which should, contrariwise, be shunned."—*Britannia.*

"'First Steps in British History' is that rarest but most valuable of all educational works—a really simple and intelligible composition, adapted to the capacities of children.   It is the best English History for schools we have yet seen."—*Critic.*

"'First Steps in British History,' being letters to a young nobleman by his tutor, is a summary of the leading events of the History of England, written in a plain, familiar style."—*Literary Gazette.*

London : J. F. Hope, 16, Great Marlborough-street.

10　　NEW WORKS PUBLISHED BY

Post 8vo, price 5s.

Christian Politics.

By the Rev. Henry Christmas, M.A., Author of "The Cradle of the Twin Giants," "Echoes of the Universe," "Shores and Islands of the Mediterranean," &c.

London: J. F. Hope, 16, Great Marlborough-street.

Second Edition, in 1 vol., double post, price 2s.

Liverpool Ho!　A Matter-of-fact Story.

By Powys Oswyn, Author of "Ernest Milman: A Tale of Manchester Life," "Ralph Deane," &c. &c.

London: J. F. Hope, 16, Great Marlborough-street.

Post 8vo, price 8s.

Julia; or, The Neapolitan Marriage.

By Margaret Tulloh.

" This work should be read by all who wish to possess a thorough knowledge of Neapolitan life."

London: J. F. Hope, 16, Great Marlborough-street.

In 1 vol., demy 8vo, price 10s. 6d.

A Ramble through the United States, Canada,

and the West Indies.　By John Shaw, M.D., F.G.S., F.L.S., Author of " A Tramp to the Diggings," &c.

" This is a most valuable work at the present time," &c.　" This book is remarkable."—*Press.*

London: J. F. Hope, 16, Great Marlborough-street.

Post 8vo, 1 vol., price 2s.　(Cheap Second Edition.)

Ernest Milman: a True Tale of Manchester

Life.　By P. Oswyn, Author of " Ralph Deane," &c.

" This work will doubtless be eagerly sought after."—*Manchester Spectator.*

London: J. F. Hope, 16, Great Marlborough-street.

Lately published, in 1 vol., post 8vo, price 2s. 6d., cloth 3s. 6d.

China: a Popular History, with a Chronolo-

gical Account of the most Remarkable Events from the earliest period to the present day. By Sir Oscar Oliphant, Kt.

London: J. F. Hope, 16, Great Marlborough-street.

J. F. HOPE, GREAT MARLBOROUGH-STREET.   11

Demy 8vo, price 7s. 6d., Illustrated.   Second Edition.

Lays of Love and Heroism, Legends, Lyrics,
and other Poems.   By Eleanor Darby, Author of " The Sweet South."

" The authoress is already well and favourably known to the British public by her previous publication, under the title of ' The Sweet South.' The appearance of the present volume will but call forth a repetition of those high encomiums which were so plentifully bestowed upon her former effort. The ' Lily o' Dundee' is of itself sufficient to show the distinguished abilities of the authoress, displaying, as it does, in a very high degree, her power, pathos, and poetic skill. The volume, as a whole, cannot fail to contribute very materially to the popularity of the accomplished authoress ; and it deserves a very extensive circulation."—*Morning Advertiser.*

London : J. F. Hope, 16, Great Marlborough-street.

Post 8vo, price 4s. Illustrated.

The Sweet South; or, a Month at Algiers.
By Eleanor Darby.

For the excellent Reviews of this Work see *Athenæum, Observer, Literary Gazette, Critic, Courier,* &c.

London : J. F. Hope, 16, Great Marlborough-street.

Fcap. 8vo, price 2s. 6d.

On the Search for a Dinner. By W. R. Hare.

London : J. F. Hope, 16, Great Marlborough-street.

Price 1s. 6d.

Thoughts on the Revision of the Prayer-
Book, and of the Terms of Clerical Conformity. By the Rev. J. R. Pretyman, M.A., late Vicar of Aylesbury, Bucks.

London : J. F. Hope, 16, Great Marlborough-street.

Price 3d. each, or 20s. per 100.   (Fourth Edition.)

An Elementary Religious Catechism; being
a Compendium of the chief Truths and Events revealed in the Holy Scriptures, as expounded and commemorated by the Church of England. By the Rev. Henry Kemp, M.A., Head Master of Cleobury-Mortimer Endowed Schools.

London : J. F. Hope, 16, Great Marlborough-street.

12   NEW WORKS PUBLISHED BY

Price 1s.

A Day on the Downs, by the Vale of White Horse.

London: J. F. Hope, 16, Great Marlborough-street.

Demy 8vo, price 12s. 6d.

Switzerland in 1854-5: a Book of Travel, Men, and Things. By the Rev. W. G Heathman, B.A., Rector of St. Lawrence, Exeter, late British Chaplain at Interlaken.

London: J. F. Hope, 16, Great Marlborough-street.

Post 8vo, pp. 332, price 1s. 6d. Illuminated.

The History of England in Rhyme, from the Conquest to the Restoration.

"A delightful book for children and young people."

London: J. F. Hope, 16, Great Marlborough-street.

Post 8vo, price 3s. 6d.

Reflections on the Mysterious Fate of Sir John Franklin. By James Parsons.

London: J. F. Hope, 16, Great Marlborough-street.

Post 8vo, 1 vol., price 6s.

Voyages to China, India, and America. By W. S. S. Bradshaw.

London: J. F. Hope, 16, Great Marlborough-street.

Post 8vo, 1 vol., price 4s. (Ready.)

Italy's Hope: a Tale of Florence. By John Ashford, Author of " The Lady and the Hound."

London: J. F. Hope, 16, Great Marlborough-street.

Post 8vo, price 2s.

The Lady and the Hound. By John Ashford.

London: J. F. Hope, 16, Great Marlborough-street.

J. F. HOPE, GREAT MARLBOROUGH-STREET. 13

Just ready. In 1 vol., price 3s.

Sermons and Lectures delivered in a Country
Church. By the Rev. W. J. Hathway, B.A.

London : J. F. Hope, 16, Great Marlborough-street.

Post 8vo, price 7s. 6d.

Mess-Table Stories, Anecdotes, and Pasquin-
ades, to Promote Mirth and Good Digestion. By Hoin
Sirmoon.

London : J. F. Hope, 16, Great Marlborough-street.

DR. E. LEE ON NICE AND MALAGA.

Demy 12mo, price 2s. 6d.

Nice and its Climate. With Notices of the
Coast from Genoa to Marseilles, and Observations on the
Influence of Climate on Pulmonary Consumption.

London: J. F. Hope, 16, Great Marlborough-street.

Price 1s. 6d.

The Nurse and the Nursery : being a Digest
of Important Information with regard to the Early Train-
ing and Management of Children ; together with Directions
for the Treatment of Accidents apt to occur in the Nursery,
and which every Nurse, Nursery Governess, and Mother
ought to know.

"The instructions which he conveys are expressed in plain and intelligible
terms, and no nurse or mother ought to be without them."—*Morning Post.*

London: J. F. Hope, 16, Great Marlborough-street.

Post 8vo, price 5s. (Just ready.)

Joan of Arc, and other Poems.
By Bonnore Berther.

London : J. F. Hope, 16, Great Marlborough-street.

14 NEW WORKS PUBLISHED BY

WORKS BY THE REV. JOHN DUFF SCHOMBERG, B.A.,
VICAR OF POLESWORTH.

DR. PUSEY REFUTED.
In post 8vo, 4s. cloth. (Ready.)

The Doctrine of the Holy Eucharist Investigated: Modern Innovations of its Purity Examined and brought to the test of Scripture, the Testimony of the Ancient Fathers, and the Declarations of the Church of England. By the Rev. John Duff Schomberg, B.A., Vicar of Polesworth.

London: J. F. Hope, 16, Great Marlborough-street.

Price 3d. (Just Published.)

The Pretensions of the Church of Rome to be considered Older than the Church of England, examined.

London: J. F. Hope, 16, Great Marlborough-street.

BY THE SAME AUTHOR.
Price 1s.

Protestant Catholicism; or, the Characteristics of Catholicism as inherited, and maintained, under Protest, by the Church of England.

"The reader will find that he has at his fingers' ends a mass of information and argument."—*Church and State Gazette.*

London: J. F. Hope, 16, Great Marlborough-street.

In demy 12mo, price 2s. 6d., cloth. Second Edition, with copious Additions.

Elements of the British Constitution, containing a comprehensive View of the Monarchy and Government of England. ,

"It is precisely what it professes to be, an exposition of the 'Elements of the British Constitution;' and as such it is deserving of a place in every Englishman's library, and should be early placed in the hands of every English schoolboy. It is comprehensive without being diffuse; clear in its statement of principles without cumbering the mind with details."—*Liverpool Courier.*

London: J. F. Hope, 16, Great Marlborough-street.

J. F. HOPE, GREAT MARLBOROUGH-STREET. 15

In 2 vols., large 8vo, price 10s.

The Theocratic Philosophy of English History,

Showing the Rise and Progress of the British Empire. In which the events of History are traced to their proper origin, the characters of persons whose actions have influenced the progress of Society delineated, and the overruling Providence of God vindicated.

"In this age of ephemeral publications, seldom does it fall to the lot of a reviewer to enjoy the privilege of calling public attention to a work of such profound research, written in such powerful and concise language, and presenting the result of years of patient investigation of an Almighty power unravelling the entangled web of human affairs. If to justify the ways of God to man—if to exhibit Divine benevolence educing ultimate good out of apparent evil; making 'the wrath of man to praise Him,' and overruling every event to subserve the grand designs of Providence;—if such an attempt executed by an author possessing in combination mental powers of no common order, has long been a desideratum, we are enabled to announce the completion of a task which will continue an imperishable memorial of the talent, and genius, and perseverance of Mr. Schomberg."—*Church Intelligencer.*

London: J. F. Hope, 16, Great Marlborough-street.

Crown 8vo, cloth, 5s.; extra gilt, 7s. 6d.; morocco, 10s. 6d.

Scottish Annual for 1859.

London: J. F. Hope, 16, Great Marlborough-street.
A. & C. Black, Edinburgh. Thomas Murray & Son, Glasgow.

Post 8vo, price 7s. 6d.

The Flower of the Wilderness. By W.

London: J. F. Hope, 16, Great Marlborough-street.

Just published, in 1 vol., post 8vo, price 8s.

Traces of Primitive Truth, &c., &c., &c.

A Manual for Missions. By the Rev. John Lockhart Ross, M.A. Oxon., Vicar of Avebury-cum-Winterbourne, Monkton, Wilts, Author of "The Church and the Civil Power," "Letters on Secession to Rome," &c., &c., &c.

London: J. F. Hope, 16, Great Marlborough-street.

Post 8vo, price 4s. Second Edition.

Anecdotes of the Bench and Bar.

By W. H. Grimmer.

London: J. F. Hope, 16, Great Marlborough-street.

16   J. F. HOPE, GREAT MARLBOROUGH-STREET.

THE NEW NOVEL.

Five Years of It.   By Alfred Austin.

"The characters are distinctly conceived, well discriminated, and consistently maintained, and the language is good." - *Saturday Review.*

" Mr. Austin can sustain a dialogue with animation, his sentiment is pleasing and refreshing, his *descriptive* passages spirited, and his style buoyant and polished."—*Morning Post.*

"There is a spirit and vitality about the book which argue well for the author's success."—*Athenæum.*

"To say that Mr. Austin's novel is a pleasing one—to say, which we must at once, that it is by far the best which has come from the printing press this year—would very inadequately express our opinion of its merits. It is not only the best of the season, but it is the best we have seen for many a season." —*Morning Chronicle.*

"A well-written and admirable story."—*Weekly Dispatch.*

London : J. F. Hope, 16, Great Marlborough-street.

IMPORTANT TO AUTHORS.

NEW PUBLISHING ARRANGEMENTS.

J. F. HOPE,

16, GREAT MARLBOROUGH STREET,

By his New Publishing Arrangements, CHARGES NO COMMISSION for Publishing Books Printed by him until the Author has been repaid his original outlay. And, as all Works entrusted to his care are Printed in the very best style, and at prices far below the usual charges, AUTHORS ABOUT TO PUBLISH will find it much to their advantage to apply to him.

Specimens, Estimates, and all particulars forwarded gratuitously, by return of post.